School Governors
A question and answer guide

About the author

A respected writer, speaker and school governor of long standing, Joan Sallis helped found Action for Governors' Information and Training (AGIT) and is President of the Campaign for the Advancement of State Education (CASE). She has lectured widely in the UK and overseas and, as well as writing for the *Times Educational Supplement*, she is a regular contributor to *Managing Schools Today*.

School Governors
A question and answer guide

Joan Sallis

Butterworth-Heinemann Ltd
Linacre House, Jordan Hill, Oxford OX2 8DP

$\mathcal{R}$ A member of the Reed Elsevier plc group

OXFORD LONDON BOSTON
MUNICH NEW DELHI SINGAPORE SYDNEY
TOKYO TORONTO WELLINGTON

First published 1995

British Library Cataloguing in Publication Data
Sallis, Joan
    School governors: a question and answer guide
    I. Title
    379.15310941

ISBN 0 7506 2283 0

Printed and bound in Great Britain by Clays Ltd, St Ives plc

Contents

Foreword

Some four years after the publication of Joan Sallis' first collection of readers' letters from the *Times Educational Supplement*, *School Governors: Your Questions Answered*, Joan has produced this timely new collection updated to include OFSTED and grant-maintained status, which easily matches her first attempt at producing a work with 'the immediacy and warmth of a weekly column'.

Much has changed since 1991 and some of the earlier tensions have re-emerged. Joan is realistic about the tough years which schools have had to face and admits that in some cases governors have added to the confusion.

However, through the pages which follow the reader will be alerted to Joan's support for the need for empowerment of governors, their activity and presence 'being the only hope for the values of public education as we know it'. Hence this book should be read by all the stakeholders in the education system: parents, teachers, heads, governors, LEA officers, teacher trainers.

Some 200 questions, coming not only from governors, but heads and teachers too, are dealt with in nine sections. Each section starts with a very helpful summary of key issues and just reading these summaries would provide the reader with a useful introduction to governors' responsibilities. If you want to flit idly through the pages, the title of each question and answer section is a summary of that question, and questions are clustered around similar themes: bullying, equal opportunities, budgets, staffing.

Questions such as:

'Are we a waste of time?'

'Should the head elect to be a governor?'

'When heads don't accept us?'

'My chairman thinks he's my boss'

'Must we publish home addresses?'

'What if we are classed a failing school?'

'Is a grant-maintained school a state school?'

reveal some of the inherent tensions in the education system in the late 1990s.

But this is not just a collection of whinges and grouses answered by an agony aunt. Joan's wealth of experience, commonsense and wisdom shine through the pages as she deals with every issue imaginable, from problems for head teachers who have inert governors, to governors whose heads do not value them. As a school governor herself and as someone who has championed the cause of governorship for some twenty years, Joan is realistic about relationships in governing bodies and passionate about their role.

A key to her philosophy is to be found on page 11:

'The volunteers have to learn to take in just what they need in order to understand the issue, and avoid getting indigestion. The professionals have to try very hard to strip issues of unnecessary detail and put them in plain and lively language.'

This book contains many messages about the importance of teambuilding, high expectations (today's governorships are not sinecures), governors sharing the vision, and the very real difficulties involved in being a school governor. However, the committed governor who is prepared to work at the role (and it is a vitally important role which repays nourishing and nurturing) will find as they read through these pages much useful and wise advice on topics such as sex education, equal opportunities, special educational needs, confidentiality, school ethos, 'rogue' governors, overpowerful cliques....

Joan exhorts governors to adopt a professional, not amateur, approach to their work. She is confident that they will rise to the many challenges confronting all who take an informed interest in schools today. Governors who are looking for some courage to support their convictions, say to be the lone voice in a strong lobby for grant-maintained status, are encouraged not to put up with any intimidation:

'Being too nice is often a problem. If this is your problem I recommend you to shut your eyes and think hard about the children. Better to offend an adult than damage a child.' (page 160)

From time to time governors need to remind themselves what governorship is all about. Too often governors' meetings discuss all manner of things but fail to deal with what really matters: the education of the children.

Joan writes much of relevance concerning sharing, good practice and partnership. Now partnership is a much overused, and misunderstood, slogan word. What we need to get across to the 'partners' in the system is the important message that partnership involves 'commensalism', i.e. eating at the same table, sharing the same meal, discussing as equals, not being thrown crumbs, sitting above, or below, the salt, being given a different menu or being asked to frequent a different restaurant. Pretend governing bodies are like junk food. The only hope for the future is the commensal governing body —the governing body which shares as equals.

Well reader, savour this edition. Tuck into it according to need. Do some preliminary nibbling before your next governors' meeting. Share the titbits you harvest from this rich collection!

You will be richly rewarded and you will have a much better taste for the subtleties of governing. You will also be eagerly awaiting Joan's next concoction of questions and answers around the year 2000.

Enjoy your feast.

Terry Mahoney
Head of Governor and Local Management Service
Hertfordshire LEA
February 1995

Introduction

This selection of questions school governors have asked me spans a period of over four years, from late 1990 to early 1995. It begins when the Education Reform Act was almost too new to have made much impact and ends when the 1993 Education Act has hardly sunk in. Two major Acts have been slipped in in-between, each altering radically the balance of power among the various education partners. The impact of the non-stop legislation 1980 to 1993 (seven major Acts in thirteen years, compared with three during the previous 120 years since 1870 when public education began) is such that it takes some time to adjust. The speed of change has stunned those who work in education, while those who have come to their heavy responsibilities from outside the service sometimes seem hardly to know what questions to ask.

It has been a great pleasure to be in contact with all these governors over the years. I never cease to be touched by the fresh perspective they bring, their interest and commitment, their sound good sense and their willingness to get up after a fall and try again. That justifies the faith that so many have placed in this venture in small-scale democracy. If a few offend, mostly through inexperience and misunderstanding, it is only to be expected in a role so new, and we should try not to overreact. It is also no surprise and no shame that many professionals have defended their territory with such determination: it is not easy to share, especially when the climate outside schools is so stormy and the consequences of mistakes in the new competitive world so serious.

It is interesting that there are so few questions about the revised curriculum, the new inspection arrangements, the special needs code of practice, the quiet introduction of non-elected quangos to share the control of local education. As I have said, the 1993 instalment of change has hardly been digested. Most of the questions revolve, as they did five years ago, around relationships within schools. Governors are concerned with the territorial issues and the problems of sharing responsibility with professionals. They also want help within the governing body to build a strong and trusting team out of a bunch of mixed ability, mixed experience strangers, some only briefly involved, united by interest in the school but divided often by chasms of ideology, education and class. They are bombarded with information about *what* they have to do and bewildered about how to do it. They know their responsibilities but continually ask why they are there, whom they represent, how they communicate, where are the lines they must not cross and how they will know when they have crossed them. They are right to choose these questions, because without the trust and acceptance of professionals their responsibilities will be a dead letter – and they know this. Given that trust and acceptance they learn very fast, and the questions they ask show a sure instinct for what is real and what is pretence.

There is still plenty of pretence, and when heads tell me they have no problems with the relationships I am pretty sure they have not yet begun. Of course governors have much to learn, and we must ensure that basic training starts early enough to restrain the few loose cannons who misjudge their role, behave inappropriately in schools and give the majority a bad name. I never defend governors who have exceeded their powers, but I still maintain that in the broad scheme of things it is heads who above all must change if we are to make a success of this new system.

It is heads who have the power, you see, and in any relationship needing forbearance and forgiveness it is the strong who must yield. They also have, if more of them could only see it, worlds to gain from getting the relationship right, not just fresh perspectives, robust decisions and passionate ambassadors, but an army to defend those public service values by which they themselves have lived their lives and which are often in such peril.

I am speaking about the habits of sharing good ideas instead of hiding your work like seven-year-olds doing a test; of striving always to meet all children's needs and to work hardest where the need is greatest; of wanting fair decisions among schools instead of devil-take-the-hindmost; of encouraging and building on the best instead of seeking out failure in order to punish it. I try saying to a wide variety of groups that failure avoidance is another name for success. It is the governors who best know what I mean. How many people have noticed one little miracle, the high profile special needs has among governors today? How quickly they have learnt that we neglect any needs at our peril, even some governors from thoughtless communities whose parents used to see slow learners as those who were holding their child back.

I wish I could say that I thought the tensions were easing and the relationships maturing. I am sorry to say that the questions I receive and my daily contact with governors suggests that the border skirmishes are increasing and the determination of some heads to resist change is gaining strength. It is as though those who thought it was all a bit of political window-dressing have begun to realize that governors' role is here to stay. That recognition may be the beginning of progress of course, especially if we can also get across the idea that most heads are still missing the chance to enter a new dimension of professional achievement. Collaborative working with governors is indeed a job worthy of talent.

The growth of governor training and support has been phenomenally fast and the quality is impressive. I sometimes get out and dust down the dreams I had when the Taylor Committee did its work eighteen years ago, and the recognition that some of the wildest have been achieved puts many a frustration into perspective. I will mention only three: that governors should have an attractive magazine delivered to their home; that they should have access to a local helpline; and that there should be a resource centre off school premises where they could consult key documents. These are not yet universal, but LEA training systems have brought them to many and at a total cost which is derisory compared with many educational initiatives.

The value for money in governor training is indeed almost unbelievable, partly because the networking has become so efficient but also because the task has attracted quite a few people who have not worked in hierarchical or well-funded organizations. Their world may have been that of voluntary or semi-voluntary service, adult and community education, the world where the recycled envelope and the Tesco carrier bag are matters of perverse pride, where you remember to retrieve the heavy document from the post-tray if you are meeting the recipient at a conference or your sister-in-law works with her husband. Those are mere badges (reusable of course) of the trade, but underneath is a belief that inventiveness, sharing experience and commitment will get you where a big budget alone cannot. They would like the big budget as well, of course. They often also know how to talk to people who do not have the code, and this and the inventiveness work like yeast in the mixture.

School governors have many problems – just look at Chapters 1 and 8, even after I have slashed them to their fair share of the space – but their enthusiasm and pride keep them going. Angela Rumbold when she was an education minister used to travel to work on a commuter line to Waterloo, and she often said that it seemed as though half the travellers were school governors, judging by the number who button-holed her, and they don't even care if I'm obviously busy, she said good-naturedly. I know them, too, those who will come up to me if I am reading something relevant on a train and say proudly 'I'm a school governor too.'

I hope they will all find in this book the respect they deserve.

Joan Sallis

1 Roles and relationships

This subject comes first because that is how governors see it. What are governors for? Whom do I represent and how can I communicate with them? Where are the lines I must not cross and how will I know if I have crossed them? How do I get things discussed?

Most governors are surprised to hear there have been school governors for something like six hundred years, and that their role has not really changed all that much. If you asked one at random to guess how long, he or she would probably say seven or eight years and then, after a little more consideration and remembering those prize days, oh no, since the 1944 Act perhaps.

School governors have been in the news for seven or eight years mainly because *schools* have had such greatly increased independence since then. It is the involvement in managing money and appointing staff, being in the front line on curriculum change, disputes over testing, pupil exclusions, major personnel problems, opting out, which have given reality to a role which used to be something between a best hat and a rubber stamp. Heads often forget this, and the tendency to associate the 'new' school governors with a whole lot of changes which came in with them has caused more tensions than anything else in this difficult relationship. The reduction in the power – and with it the protection – of the local authority, in the political drive to liberate schools as part of a much more market-orientated service, is a source of anxiety to many who work in education, and the messengers often get blamed for messages they did not write.

Centuries before there were schools for all, paid for from public funds, people realized that education, even as a minority activity, had an importance to society different from other goods and services. Schools nurtured those who would one day have power over us, those who would teach our children and heal our diseases, and those who would paint and write and make music to delight future generations. They also had quite a lot to do with how people behaved. Therefore we all needed to be vigilant, even if they were not our children in there. School governors under different names were therefore introduced to guard the public interest – the watchdog role – and to bring the perspectives of the home, the workplace and the streets, the light of ordinariness if you like, to bear on an expert activity which could otherwise easily become remote – the partner-cum-critical-friend role. That has not changed essentially. The powers which schools have have increased and the range of people thought of as potential school governors has increased. Not much else.

School governors have always on paper played a major part in appointing the head, managing the budget, overseeing the curriculum and settling disputes. They also had a general public relations role. So it is now. If these responsibilities were not taken seriously, it was partly because school governorship was dominated first by local worthies and increasingly then by political parties, and partly because the school was guided and supported in these roles by the LEA. The introduction of parent, teacher and community governors, and the delegation of many functions to schools alone, put school governors in the limelight.

School governors now have sole responsibility for appointing the head and deputy head. They are also responsible for all other staff appointments, but they may delegate this responsibility as they wish. They determine the curriculum of the individual school, within the limits of the national curriculum and any local constraints, that is to say what is taught and the general organization of its teaching, not of course the detail of how pupils are taught. They manage the budget, though they will undoubtedly wish to keep this to a broad responsibility with enough flexibility allowed for the smooth management of the school. They decide the staffing complement – numbers, grades and, within certain national limits, pay. They have the personnel functions of an employer, though the LEA remains employer in law. They have care of the premises and decide their use outside school hours. They determine whether a permanently excluded pupil should be reinstated or not. They must report to parents once a year, and arrange an annual meeting for parents to discuss the report and the running of the school. They are also responsible for ensuring parents get all the information they are entitled to. Within their general curriculum responsibility they have specific responsibility for religious education and worship, sex education, and the identification of and provision for special educational needs.

These are strategic, not day-by-day management roles, and inexperienced governors sometimes get themselves into hot water by intervening in the school at too detailed a level. They may simply misunderstand their role and wish to be active and involved. On the other hand they are occasionally frustrated by failure to involve them at a level which *is* appropriate or by the disregard, in the name of day-by-day-management, of governors' decisions.

The head teacher's role is to manage the school day-by-day, being responsible for the use of the school's resources of time, space and people to best advantage. The head is also responsible for the professional performance of staff and their professional development and for the maintenance of an ordered environment in which learning can take place. This means responding to breaches of that order from any source on a day-to-day basis. He or she is also the governors' chief professional adviser.

A new head: how to make a good start on the relationship

 We start the school year with a newly-appointed head. The last one retired after twenty years in the school, and although he was caring and conscientious, he never managed to accept the new powers of governors and we didn't quite frankly ever assume our proper role. One had to feel sorry for him, as his familiar world had vanished and he found the whole business of 'open government' stressful. I was one of the governors who took part in the appointment process, and we were determined this time to appoint someone who was prepared to work in a more collaborative mode. Have you any hints on how to embark on the new relationship? I am a fairly experienced parent governor (and was chair) and hope to be re-elected, and we have only had about 25% change, but it's still quite hard starting with so many unknowns.

 It is hard, but it is an opportunity many would envy as you realize. It was interesting that you said how much weight was given to 'governor-friendly' qualities in appointing this time, after a fairly difficult experience: I am sure we shall see that repeated often in future.

I have no doubt you are aware of the danger that in your anxiety to assume 'your proper role' you will go to extremes and frighten your new head away from his collaborative stance. The first thing to establish is that you are a group of friendly and supportive people who don't want to run his school but who will respond well to being allowed to turn their commitment to the school into a genuine sharing of responsibility. It might be a good idea if you could organize some kind of social gathering (if only for a short time before the scheduled meeting) for him to get to know you informally. As outgoing chair you should at least make an opportunity to have a friendly talk to him yourself and concentrate first on finding out what *his* priorities are and second on exploring how he thinks governors can best involve themselves in the life of the school. You must strike a balance between establishing your space as governors and making a satisfying and appropriate amount of space for him.

More formally, the first full meeting of governors does need some planning if you are to start as you mean to go on. I often stress how important it is to look ahead and not just be agenda-driven. The best way to ensure that governors are not only invoked after the event is to see the events coming. With a new head I would attach special importance to an initial discussion of the issues which will have to be addressed in the school in the coming year. Talk to him about this beforehand so that he can organize his own thoughts and lead the item. It is important, though, to structure things so that governors have a chance to react, to bring up points of their own and to contribute to a shared understanding of the wider agenda.

That naturally leads to how governors are going to plan their year, and to a discussion of some acceptable system for them all to have a chance to observe the school at work. Stress that the object of this is learning, not interfering or judging. Wise, too, I think, to allay fears and head off possible trouble by talking about ground rules for governors visiting school, since while nobody wants to restrict any governor's enthusiasm, courtesy and discretion must be observed. New governors may need this caution, and having the discussion openly and early on will give a good message to the head. So will some reminder to yourselves that governors' responsibility is corporate, that as individuals you have no power, and that every governor must accept and be loyal to decisions made by the group. Trouble is often caused by governors trying to exert influence as individuals. With a fresh start like this it is also important to talk a bit about information sharing, and the most efficient way in which governors can be prepared for the strategic decisions they have to make. The best guarantee of being involved is to have the proper structure for involvement already in place, with fair and efficient work-sharing.

You must just assume that your new head will want such involvement, not in a threatening way but as a matter of course. But again I must stress, don't forget that he will have a vision about how he wants the school to develop and you must encourage him to express that vision and share it. Even in the matter of relationships with you, it is far better if ideas come from him, and if he leaves the first meeting feeling that the development of the governing body as an effective team is a management task in which he can take professional pride.

Frustrated, but willing to try again

 After much heart-searching during my summer holiday I have decided to offer myself again for election as a parent governor. I was not one of the ones who was put off by the workload – I am deeply interested in the school and will do whatever is required – but I found it full of pretence. I won't go into all the reasons and in trying again I am obviously accepting that with my experience I can perhaps do a better job for parents this time round. But everything we were ever asked to comment on was a foregone conclusion and I cannot say we had a real share in any decisions other than to approve them after the event. Debate was never encouraged by the head and in this he was backed up by our chairman who either just wanted a quiet life or had been squared beforehand, or both. I was made to feel a trouble-maker if I raised anything parents were concerned about or even made a practical suggestion for governors to support the school. I often wondered what a meeting had achieved which could not be achieved without us. Any tips please on how to move things on?

 You are asking for a whole book by way of answer as I expect you know! Nor will you be surprised to hear that I have a file of questions from summer beaches all on different aspects of the pretend governing body and how to make it real, so your problem will be much in evidence in the weeks to come. I know that there are thousands of schools where governors play a full and satisfying part, but the evidence of the number where the sharing has scarcely begun is depressing. To be positive, schools have had a tough few years and must often have got themselves through weariness or inexperience into unproductive relationships which many participants must now in this breathing space want to improve. I hope there will be others like you wanting a new start, and that these will include some head teachers.

Do you know any other governors who are hoping to continue to be or become governors in your school with whom you could talk things through in these vital weeks? You need some allies to get things on a better basis, and a plan for the first meeting. Looking one more step ahead, can you think of any likely new co-opted governors who might bring new life to the group and whom you could (with their permission) suggest?

There are a number of important things to try for in the first full meeting which will not happen if you miss this chance. The first of course is to elect a chair who will be a team-builder and who is capable of a relationship with the head which is both productive and non-exclusive of others. So often we just sit and let this vital 'election' just happen. It is a good idea to start by talking about the qualities you all want in a chair before you do it, and to have sounded out and discussed with colleagues any likely takers.

The second thing is to make sure governors look ahead at that meeting to some of the issues that face the school. Ask the head to lead you on this (as an experienced governor you can suggest this, telling him in advance that you are going to do so): it makes the point that governors have a role other than to rubber-stamp and that they must plan their work accordingly. At the same time check that everyone knows the process of getting things on the agenda and that you have an understanding with the head on how to deal with concerns brought to you by parents.

Then to planning the work. It is essential that governors grasp this role – otherwise they will always be dragged along behind events. You need to discuss how you can effectively break up the work so that it gets prepared in more depth by small groups, making sure that all governors are involved in tasks of equal importance so as to avoid A and B teams.

Finally, you must establish a system by which each governor gets some regular experience of the school at work, either by a month of duty, or taking a subject interest, or being attached to a class or year. Without this your decisions won't be so good even if you get to make them.

All these suggestions can be discussed in advance with the head and other governors. You may well find that you are not the only one who is waiting for a chance to improve things.

When heads don't accept us

 The question I'm sure you get asked most often is why some head teachers are so reluctant to accept governors' new role, and how governors can cope with defensiveness and even hostility. Perhaps some governors are lucky enough to have open relationships and real participation, but listening to what others say at training evenings I would say there are many who are having problems as well. It will drive governors away in the end. I wonder if those who'll accept such a frustrating role will be as much use to schools as those who won't?

 That last question is a good one and I hope any heads who read your words will take it to heart. To deal with this issue fully would need a book. But first we must all accept that change takes time and patience, and indeed that many heads who have worked in a particular way for a long time will be secretly hoping that if *they* are patient this particular change will go away! Therefore we must look for ways of persuading the latter group that governors are: (a) here to stay; (b) legitimate; (c) the only hope for the values of public education as we know it; and (d) the greatest test of professional leadership. Although (a), (b) and (c) are powerful, I really think (d) may be the trump card because it appeals to professional pride. Every governor can do something to promote these arguments.

Then we must be well-behaved, recognizing the proper level of our involvement at a strategic level and not meddling. We must accept that individually we have no power – only the governing body has power, and our strength is in team effort. We must understand the reasons why sharing is hard – the stress and intolerable pace of change in schools, which makes people tense and reluctant to delegate; the need to shuffle off bad memories of governors of the past with no commitment, private agendas, and sometimes a leaning to the interests of the privileged; and a genuine difficulty in seeing governors as a group suitable for development, instead of a cause for relief if not too bad, and despair if awful.

I believe LEAs have a duty to help more than they do. After all if, in future, good education depends on relationships, it is foolish to ignore warning signs and wait for a crisis. Whatever the future holds, LEAs still have a duty to support schools in their care.

Heads, once motivated, have a worthwhile task of helping to

build teams, which are made, not born. It is only heads' commitment to partnership which can lead them to share values, provide the raw material for good decisions, develop ambassadors who are beyond price. All we can do is try to prove in every way we know that we care about the school, especially those in it who find life hard; that debate is healthy and not threatening; and that we are prepared to be patient. Don't give up – as you so rightly say, our successors will otherwise demonstrate that blind support is not worth having.

Frustration not exhaustion

 I read a lot in the press about governors resigning because of the heavy load of responsibility. Maybe I am not typical, but I am not the only one on my governing body and others in our LEA to say that I am ready to work as hard for the school as I am allowed, but many of us are frustrated because we are the victims of a form of benevolent suffocation.

First the LEA behaves as though it was twenty years ago and governors were just a front for their somewhat extreme policies. We are continually being bombarded with long-winded ideology and in effect told what to do. Our agendas come from the town hall and there is no school input whatsoever. They are boring and not relevant and don't give us any sense of achievement when we have ploughed through and rubber-stamped the proposals. Within the school things are no better. The budget is delegated in name only: all we do is approve it when everything has been decided, and the same is true of the curriculum, pupil discipline, etc. The head writes the annual report to parents and runs the meeting. Parents don't say a word: they have not been used to it. Once or twice we have tried to establish our right to an opinion where we have felt really strongly (such as on one exclusion case) but we were made to feel disloyal and told by the head that teachers would strike if we intervened and that the LEA would support them. If I resign it will be because of things like this.

 I am glad you have written. What you describe may sound like another world to many governors who have run their own meetings for years, where head and governors are largely managing on their own and governors genuinely share responsibility. Yet I believe that, if not typical, yours is the experience of a significant number of governors, and their justified disillusionment could wreck the system. The problem mostly arises in a few urban or suburban metropolitan authorities and the odd county, where one party or the other has been secure for a long time. I don't believe that power ever lies on the floor for long: if it is allowed to slide from governors' laps it will soon be picked up, with dangerous consequences.

That is why I hope that you and others like you *will* go on. You have made progress because you know what you are up against, and should not hand over to another lot of innocents. LEAs are only bluffing when they seek to control governors' business, and the sad part is that in many cases LEAs like that breed heads like yours. They also fuel opposition to LEAs generally and they miss opportunities to develop a more worthwhile role.

It sounds as if you are not the only person on your board who is fed up, so muster what support there is to allow the school to assume the role the law intends. No big bust-up is needed. Quietly establish a routine for framing your own meetings schedule and agenda (with individuals encouraged to contribute) and make it clear that the LEA are welcome to suggest items (indeed there are many things they are legally obliged to refer to all governors). But it is your agenda, your meeting, your chair, your clerk, and you can build the meeting around what *you* think important. 'You' in this case including the head who stands to benefit greatly from your making a stand if he could only shake off habits based on fear. Assure him of your goodwill and show it.

The next stage is to plan your work so as to encompass the budget, curriculum, discipline, staffing issues you should be addressing, and plan for writing co-operatively your next annual report. Address yourselves to questions of communication with parents more generally. Planning is the key: if you do these things you will not be at the mercy of the *fait accompli*. The kind of policies you are up against thrive on governors' inertia and lack of foresight. Try not to make your head feel that he is the object of your change of tactics. See if somebody he listens to can spell out how the regime he has become part of demotivates people. Support him where you can. If you have not elected a chair for this year make sure it is somebody who is in sympathy with this way of working. You might be helped by some big whole-school project which would be independent of the LEA and would be a good team-building venture, preferably something close to the head's interests.

How can I share responsibility with my governors?

 As a head I try hard to keep my governors well-informed and to seek their views. I am genuinely bewildered about how I can share the responsibility of the school in any meaningful way or build understanding relationships with a group of people – pleasant, well-intentioned, sensible I grant you - whom I meet infrequently, whose knowledge of school routines is minimal, and who haven't the time, willing as they are, to read the volume of paper necessary to understand every issue.

 You have a good start: you want the relationship to succeed. In everyday life we find the proper level of communication for a range of vastly different relationships without any trouble. Why is the relationship dealt with here so difficult? I think it is because heads and their professional colleagues know so much about the *process* of education that they find it hard to imagine that people who don't and can't know so much do know what its purposes are, can help to judge outcomes and, most important, advise and warn on how policies will go down in the school community.

I am glad you have expressed this concern, because the relationship between professionals and volunteers engaged on the same enterprise, whatever its character, face the same problem, and I know that it is difficult to find, as we do in other relationships, the right level of communication. Often intense commitment is shared but detailed knowledge can't be. The volunteers have to learn to take in just what they need in order to understand the issue, and avoid getting indigestion. The professionals have to try very hard to strip issues of unnecessary detail and put them in plain and lively language.

Ensure that your governors do all the small-group work that the law and their time allow. Ensure that they spend time on a regular and committed basis in classrooms: even a little brings a lot of understanding that hours of reading couldn't achieve, but the activity must be selected and planned. Think of things that give a feel of the school, like newsletters, and see that governors get them (a simple and cheap way is to have a folder for each governor in school, and have the office slip in each a copy of everything that goes out by child: the governor must call and empty it). Get a few governors invited to key staff meetings sometimes, but first give them a list of the technical terms and acronyms likely to occur on the subject concerned, with definitions. Use teachers, especially skilled communicators, to bring insights to governors' meetings.

To get the level of governor involvement right, try to bring them in more at the brainstorming, not the carefully argued paper, stage. They have a good idea what the object of a pay or behaviour or charging policy ought to be even if they can't write one. They also probably know when it is not working. Do use them as a sounding-board for anything with a likely dramatic impact on the school's users. To give some examples, the arguments for vertical grouping, changing from mixed ability to streaming or vice versa, dropping Latin, changing from separate to combined science, going over to a 'real books' policy, are highly complex and technical. But your 'pleasant, well-intentioned, sensible' group will know instantly, without any closely argued papers, that these changes are going to be hard to sell to many people, and why, and you will need all your skill to select for them the arguments they need on both sides. You may also find it helpful to share out any really difficult papers that you can't protect them from, letting each governor research and present one issue.

You do need to learn how to use a broad brush if this relationship is not going to lead to despair. Governors are not there to limp behind in every detailed process of running a school, but to share a vision for it, consent to the means of realizing that vision, and help you judge the results. There is no need to feel that you are patronizing them if you try to keep your communication on this level as long as you respect, as I am sure you do, that they bring skills and experience that the school needs and that their perspective is equal in value to that of the educator.

Is it my job to ensure that my governors understand their role?

 As a head I am concerned that my governors know very little about their role though they have enough opinions to fill a tabloid newspaper. They don't go to any training sessions, of which plenty are provided in different neighbourhoods. It seems almost farcical that they have such serious responsibilities when they are so abysmally ill-informed about the school, the education system and their own job as governors. I don't consider it is my job to train them and I can't insist that they undertake training. Any advice please?

 Some people think formal training should be compulsory, but it is not. I don't believe we should consider making it compulsory until the range and quality are as good everywhere as the best now on offer (which is superb), even if it were thought desirable.

In many schools a good deal of informal learning goes on with the head as a gentle guide. The school is in some ways the best base for learning, and governors who seem poorly motivated often become enthusiastic when they know the school better. I strongly recommend you to institute some system for involving every governor in some observation of the school – governor of the month, governor attached to a class or subject. But you must be pleasantly persistent about it and not let people slide out. You might also have a word with your local governor training team and see if they could organize some kind of training workshop within your school.

It *is* serious that your governors don't take advantage of what is on offer, especially as you say elsewhere in your letter that they have paid for the 'package' from their own training funds. Have you pointed out the significance of this waste of money? I assume that as a governor you do regularly go to training sessions yourself, and keep trying to encourage governor colleagues to come with you? Could you get training put on the agenda of each meeting and ask who has been to what?

But then you say at some length in your letter that you don't think it is your job and quite a lot of resentment comes through. I sympathize, but I am bound to say too that I think you should ask who suffers most if you don't get involved, who will benefit if you do, and who will if you don't. Also relationships will deteriorate as your negative feelings increase and become more apparent.

I think the key word for you is expectations. I am sure you have high expectations of your staff. You will have every trick in the professional book for pleasantly communicating them. You have high expectations of pupils, too, and in dealing with children, as a parent or a teacher, it is mostly bluff, because there is not a lot you can do if they decide not to respond. But they do. Could you manage to think of governors in this context? Governors are a motley group with growth potential like any other and respond to leadership. The trouble is that I don't think you have yet seen them as a suitable case for leadership.

My chairman thinks he is my boss

I am a head teacher. My chairman of governors seems to think he is my line manager. He visits every Monday morning and wants me to clear my plans for the week with him. He establishes what he sees to be my priorities. He asks me to contact him if I need to go to a meeting off-site, and on the odd occasion he has said that he does not think that meeting is as important as X, Y, or Z in the school. Do I have to put up with this?

This is serious, not just for you but for the proper development of governors as the law intended and for their reputation. The tiny number of cases like yours I hear about gives us all a bad name, and the fact that there are so few is no comfort to you.

This governor has totally misunderstood his role and is involving himself in the daily management of the school. He is also usurping the role of the governing body by presuming to act on their behalf without direction from them. The chair has no power on his own, except in an emergency, and even the whole governing body is not there to line-manage the head.

You need help to deal with this. I would be surprised if you felt there was any point in fighting it head-on or any chance of getting other governors to discipline this dangerously confused colleague, so I suggest you ask your LEA to speak to your chair. Whom you ask will depend in part on what sort of governor he is. If he represents the LEA then maybe you should go to your chair of the education committee, which will have appointed him. It will also depend on whom you know and feel comfortable with in your local system. The county director of education, most probably, or your area officer. I believe the LEA should deal with such threats to good working relationships in a much more proactive way than most do. Show the person you approach your letter to me and this reply if it helps. It would be useful also to send it to the person responsible for your governor training: such matters should be covered in training, but of course training is voluntary! Maybe they could arrange some team training for your whole governing body so that the chair cannot escape it. Or put something in their governors' magazine about what chairs of governors should *not* be doing!

I hope this experience will not lead you to underrate the strength that a properly-working governing body can be to you and the school, or diminish your will to involve governors at the proper strategic level. That would really be letting this idiot get the better of you.

What can they do to us if we make illegal decisions?

 Quite often you say that something governors have told you goes on in their school is not legal. What sanctions can such illegal actions give rise to, who applies them, and what is governors' liability? The rules and regulations are so complicated that it would be a miracle if we were all working to them in my view.

 Yes, I would say that every day somewhere a governing body is innocently making decisions in ways not strictly legal. We are in an evolutionary process and so this is not surprising. No action is likely to be taken on the great majority of minor breaches because there are too many lawbreakers and not enough police! Anyway the fact that a decision is not made in the proper way does not necessarily mean it is in itself a *wrong* decision, and often nobody can say what a particular bit of the law means for sure until it is challenged in the courts. The danger arises when there is an aggrieved party with the motivation – and the resources, either personally or through the backing of a professional association or other organization – to challenge a decision which has not been properly made. An unsuccessful candidate for a job, the parents of an excluded pupil, a teacher involved in disciplinary proceedings, teachers unwilling to teach a reinstated pupil after exclusion are easy examples, and governors must always take special care when justice to individuals might be in question. These are far more likely to rebound than, say, voting in a co-opted governor with a quorum of less than two-thirds or taking a decision on a governors' committee on a subject which cannot legally be delegated. Yet even these are important since such breaches allow decisions to be made by too few people.

You ask what could happen. Well, sometimes there is provision for an appeal to an outside body (an industrial tribunal, or a special appeals board on exclusion from school) which has power to reverse the original decision, either on its merits or because it was irregularly made. Or an injured party could take the matter either to the Department for Education, who can direct governors (or an LEA) to reverse some policy, or to the courts, who can render a decision invalid. Governing bodies cannot be dismissed or have their powers removed unless they have grossly mismanaged the school. As for financial liability for a decision which goes wrong, the 1988 Act says that governors are not individually liable for the consequences of any action taken in good faith, which the Department for Education say means 'honestly and without ulterior motive', and the incorporation of governing bodies in April 1994 gave individual governors further protection. Serious financial consequences for the *school* could arise from decisions successfully challenged, e.g. a wrongful dismissal, but even here the LEA foots the bill in an LEA school if it supported the original decision. So while I would not want any governing body to be other than serious about doing things properly and willing to learn, I would not want hard-pressed governors to be sleepless either.

Are we a waste of time?

 Our headmistress is very firm on the question of the internal management of the school being her affair and not ours. But some of her recent actions make nonsense of the things which are our job, like the development plan, the staffing and especially the budget.

For instance, we have just discovered that she had dispensed with a teacher on a temporary contract even though provision had been made in the agreed budget for this post and we would have wanted it to be made permanent. It was a science specialist what is more, precious in a

primary school, and a good teacher. We had said many times that when we had the opportunity in the school we must replace a few 'generalist' class teachers with specialists in science, technology and music. The last teacher she appointed was someone without these specialisms.

Another example is in our charging policy. We had said that we did not want to have any pupils excluded even from out-of-school activities which were not essential to the curriculum. Parents raise funds to enable all pupils to participate in treats and anyway as governors we said that we would sooner the treat didn't take place than that any child was excluded. Yet she wrote to parents about a theatre outing at half-term and said she was afraid they could not go if they did not pay.

Finally we had put in our behaviour guidelines that no punishment should be embarrassing to the child, and now we have heard she has made girls wear boys' caps if they are caught fighting, and also boys and girls wear paper hats saying 'I bite' or 'I tell lies', etc. I sometimes think we are a waste of time.

Almost every week I hear about head teachers taking actions in what they consider day-by-day management which conflict with decisions they have shared as governors.

You are right in all that you say. Those actions should not have been taken in contravention of policies agreed. I hope that you will not let them pass, but be pleasant, since it *is* difficult for people who have been used to acting without real involvement of governors for so long to adapt to new ways of working. I should guess that your head is not young, from the style of the examples you give. Please realize we all have to be patient and that change takes time. It is a good thing if general policies and plans are reviewed routinely from time to time as a reminder of what was agreed, and if examples can be given on, e.g. the outings and the punishments, of the kind of things you had in mind. Governors should not abdicate their responsibility for appointments of staff. If you had proper arrangements to be represented on every interviewing panel, and made sure they were observed, some of your concerns could be dealt with. And by the way I am not sure that I like the suggestion that it is all right for boys to fight and not girls!

Splitting and reorganizing classes: is it an issue for governors?

Our head teacher has had to split the reception class because new housing has increased our numbers through the school but especially at the bottom end. Of course we accept this and the parents of those children are delighted, especially as the new class will take the younger entrants so no child will be moved. Because we have not space or staffing to do this operation without further reorganization, however, the junior classes have been reduced from four to three with the older pupils in each group having to move up. There has been an outcry among parents about this and some of us on the governing body feel we should at least have been warned since we are under great pressure. The head has been quite nasty, saying it is his job to manage the school. Should we have been brought into this? We can now afford to get another teacher but the head wants to make this a specialist appointment for science and technology throughout the school.

Establishing two reception classes in itself could be called day-by-day management, but reorganizing age (or ability) groups on any scale does, in my view, come into a big 'dark-grey' area which should involve governors. This is because of its likely effect on parents, who in general heartily dislike any messing around with their children's teaching groups. It therefore needs such careful presentation that it is wise to plan and discuss it thoroughly, not only getting the backing of governors but also explaining the problem to parents and reassuring them.

I don't know enough about the circumstances to say whether this was a wise move, but on the face of it it looks as if you are going to have undesirably large classes throughout the school before long (even if you have not now) and you urgently need to plan for this, either by acquiring extra accommodation or restricting admissions. Parents need reassuring, not just that the present hand-to-mouth solutions are unavoidable and workable, but that adequate provision will be made as these two reception classes move through the school. As for the new appointment, while I can't comment on how that post should be used, I should have thought governors ought to have been involved in that decision too and indeed that it should have formed part of their long-term staffing strategy within the school development plan.

Can the head stop us forming a parents' association?

 Campaigners and journalists are always saying the head can stop parents forming an association. Is this really true? Where does it say this?

 A good question and I am not sure that I can answer it. I have also shouted from time to time about parents' right to form an association based on the school and I signed the Taylor Report, which recommended seventeen years ago that it should be a legal right. This is also the official policy of the National Confederation of PTAs, of CASE, of the Labour Party and many others. I still think the legitimacy of parents' associating together in a school should be explicitly enshrined in law whatever the present legalities, which I *think* are these.

Nobody can prevent parents setting up an association of course. They can meet off school premises. And since governors are responsible for the use of school premises outside school hours it is for them to decide who meets in the school. If it is to be a parent–*teacher* association, so that the co-operation of the head and staff are needed, that is different. If any reader disagrees with this or has anything helpful to add I would be most grateful.

What I *am* sure of is that there are not many governing bodies who would facilitate a parents' association by agreeing to its meeting in the school if the head were publicly antagonistic, and if they did the association would suffer from the lack of recognition by and support from the head. This is where an explicit statement of right would help, and that would presumably also override the governors' powers.

Role of governors in an aided school

 I have just been appointed a 'foundation' governor of a voluntary-aided school. I am afraid I am very ignorant about what this means: I am just an ordinary member of the village community and all my children attend the school: it is in fact the only school in the village. Do I have any special role, and whom should I ask about my duties? Why are governing bodies of church schools different?

 Your final question is a big one and you need to go back a long way in history to answer it, but as many governors are interested I'll do my best. Voluntary-aided schools - the great majority either Church of England or Roman Catholic - were originally provided by a voluntary body, but they were integrated into the state system of education by stages in 1870, 1902 and 1944, and the LEA pay the teachers and all the day-by-day running costs. Aided schools, apart from providing religious education and worship in their own faith, have the same general curriculum and observe the same rules as county schools, i.e., those provided by local authorities.

Aided schools do, however, still retain some responsibility (in particular for maintaining the outside of the building) and have some corresponding privileges compared with county schools. The main ones are the right of the founding body to appoint a majority on the governing board (the choice is up to them), and a say about which children get preference if the school is oversubscribed. The governors are also legally the employers of the staff, though the LEA pay salaries. In practice this is not now very different from county schools, where the governors have the personnel functions even though they are not employers. To complete the story, there are also voluntary-controlled schools, which couldn't afford the responsibilities of an aided school in 1944 when they had the choice: these are more like county schools in the structure of their governing bodies and don't have any financial obligations. They do, however, provide denominational worship and religious education.

Your role as a foundation governor is in most ways just the same as any other governor. Whatever interest group we represent, we all share equally in the legal responsibilities of governors and owe our first loyalty to the school and its well-being. But we all bring distinctive experience to bear and a point of view which reflects where we are coming from. All governors of voluntary schools, and especially perhaps the foundation governors, must protect the school's distinctive religious character and see that any special requirements in the trust deed under which the school was established are honoured. For instance, in a Roman Catholic school the trust deed might say that the sanctity and permanence of marriage should be upheld: there might then be a problem of appointing a divorced and remarried candidate to a senior post.

I am sure your vicar will gladly talk to you about your role if you want to know any more, but the appointing body will have made a conscious decision to include ordinary people from the school community so I am sure you won't have any problems.

Governors who leave all decisions to the head

Some heads complain to you about governors overstepping the mark. And many governors say heads won't let them assume their proper role. My problem is getting my governors to accept their responsibilities at all! They are conscientious and supportive, but wish to defer to me in the end on all matters requiring a policy decision: 'You are the professional,' they say. I would welcome shared decisions in these difficult times to strengthen the school. Can you advise?

I see that your school is in a remote rural area, and the tradition of respect for the head teacher is possibly even more persistent than it is in the population as a whole. Perhaps you should first be pleased that you enjoy such trust. In general you can only remind governors that certain matters are their legal responsibility and assure them that you genuinely want them to exercise it.

More particularly, it is worth saying that in all probability you run the school in a way that inspires your governors' complete confidence. If you introduced something which they sensed would be controversial in your community – the abandoning of a graded reading scheme, for instance – you might find that you picked up their unease pretty quickly and also that they soon learned to challenge you.

Perhaps, however, much as you want to share, you come over without knowing it as very confident and self-sufficient. That is daunting for people feeling their way. Try to let some of your human weakness show. Being needed is more motivating than being wanted.

There are other things you can do, anyway, to make them more active participants. First, don't always bring things to them in a too thought-through and polished form. It is natural for professionals not to want to go public on a proposal until it is as perfect as they can make it, but it inhibits people. Get into the habit of thinking aloud with them, and sometimes share a problem to which you genuinely don't have an answer. Give small groups of governors issues to worry out on their own, and share out the brown envelopes, letting an individual have the first sight of a paper to make what they can of and bring to the meeting with further information and recommendations. Make sure you have a system for involving every governor in some observation of the school at work or some responsibility. Be certain that the minutes of decisions clearly attribute decisions to governors.

Because you stress their commitment I have assumed throughout that there is nothing wrong with your governors themselves except excessive modesty and the habits of a lifetime. If, however, some of your LEA or foundation appointees are elderly, remote from children and the ways of a modern primary school, do be brave enough to ask the appointing body to consider younger people from the community, perhaps ex-parent governors, or people from other agencies concerned with children, when they re-appoint.

Heads and governors: drawing the white lines

 I know it is not easy or helpful to try to draw rigid lines between the responsibilities of head and governors, but I should like your opinion on the following actions taken by head teachers without consultation in the course of a year in a group of schools whose governors meet informally to exchange ideas: (a) changing to a completely new reading scheme for which incidentally no provision had been made in the budget – the money came from the contingency fund; (b) adopting mixed age classes in the junior department to help accommodate a bulging infants

*intake; (c) deciding to cut a post (by not advertising a vacancy); (d)
abolishing head of year posts and instead going to head of upper and
lower school positions; (e) suspending a teacher for a suspected
misdemeanour, pending investigation; (f) exchanging two class teachers
to broaden their experience; (g) switching two sections of
accommodation in terms of their curriculum use; (h) deciding, following
parental protests, to drop sex education for one age group of young
juniors. All these heads think they are good at sharing responsibility.*

 Yes, a long way to go. Sad, since many of these actions are
controversial in terms of public opinion – changing reading
schemes and going to mixed age groups, switching teachers,
abolishing familiar posts – and a wise head would make sure of
some well-informed ambassadors before embarking on them,
whatever the legal demarcation might be judged to be. In strictly
territorial terms I should say that (a), (b), (c), (d) and (h)
unquestionably required governors' decisions: (a) because it is
a major curriculum change and also because the switch of funds
would almost certainly exceed the amount governors had
agreed should be within the head's discretion, (b) and (c)
because they are major and sensitive organizational changes at
a strategic level, (d) because governors decide on the staffing
complement, and (h) because governors have clear
responsibility for sex education and parental comments should
be addressed to them for reply or action. On (e), either the head
or the governors may legally suspend a teacher, but if a major
disciplinary action seems to be looming, a head would be wise
to keep close to governors. (f) and (g) I would regard as day-by-
day management issues, but if they are likely to cause parental
concern, sharing thoughts with governors would be sensible.

You are right to say that hard lines are not helpful: there must
be give and take and an evolutionary approach to changing
long-undisturbed autonomy. At the same time, there is a clear
area of strategic decision making which arises from governors'
responsibility for curriculum and staffing policy and budget
allocation. Governors who are involved in such strategic areas
are much less likely to 'meddle' in routine management matters,
especially if the head has earned their trust by ensuring that
agreed policies are not infringed in the name of day-by-day
management.

What if you see something worrying when visiting the school?

 If, as a visiting governor, you see something that concerns you, something quite serious, is it all right to raise it under any other business at the next governors' meeting? I am thinking of things like a class hopelessly out of control, a teacher shouting and smacking. I did that and I got a terrible telling off from the chairman and the head has not spoken to me since. I did tell the teacher I was going to report it. What is the good of going on a tour of inspection if you can't take any action?

 An individual governor has no power to take action. It is only the governing body which can act. I'm also a bit worried about your talking of a tour of inspection. Governors don't visit schools in the role of inspector. What you did was wrong on two grounds. First, if you criticize an individual in a meeting that person must have a chance to be present and to bring a friend. That is natural justice. If in such a case the teacher was eventually dismissed, an industrial tribunal might rule wrongful dismissal because the first complaint had been made without those safeguards, and that would be very costly. Second, a governor should never raise a serious matter at a meeting without first warning the head and also seeking the chair's permission. It is putting both at a disadvantage.

Do not misunderstand. I am not saying you should say nothing. It *is* serious if a teacher loses control to the extent of smacking a child, because that is against the law, and you should not even wait for a meeting. Since the teacher could get into trouble, the head should certainly know about the matter at once. You should have mentioned it to him the same day, in private. I should be surprised if he did not know there was a problem with that teacher, but perhaps not how serious. One won't always be popular, of course, for bringing unwelcome news, but the important thing is that it should be dealt with and you will have to settle for that. A good technique is to say: 'I know you will have procedures for handling these things so I'll leave it with you. Perhaps you could just reassure me some time that it is under control.' That puts the management of the issue squarely where it belongs, shows that you don't want to interfere, but gives just a hint that you won't drop it.

2 Membership of governing bodies

Although there have been governing bodies of some kind for six hundred years or so, there was, until 1980, no clear indication of the kind of people who were to be members. References are made in old documents to eminence in the worlds of science, letters and business, but what these amounted to in essence was 'worthy' and 'suitable'. In other words there was no representative or popular element. With the much greater emphasis in the 1960s and 1970s on consumer influence in general and with the growth of parents' movements in education and the development of comprehensive schools, there was growing pressure for parent and teacher representation at least, and some LEAs responded to it. Indeed, during the 1970s about 90% introduced some representation of such interests, but on a token scale. This was somewhat stimulated by local government reorganization in 1974.

The Taylor Committee was set up in 1975 to look into the whole question of school decision making and accountability, and its report, *A New Partnership for our Schools*, recommended in 1977 that all schools should have individual governing bodies, and that in county schools at least they should be an equal partnership of four interests – LEA, parents, teachers and community – sharing in all school policy decisions and with overall responsibility for communication with parents and the public.

The Education Act of 1980 was a timid response to these recommendations providing that all schools, county and voluntary, should have two parent governors and one or two teacher governors, depending on the size of school. No guidance was given as to the composition of the rest of the governing body so of course it was still open to the LEA to appoint a majority.

In 1986, however, a new Education Act implemented most of the Taylor recommendations, and set out a standard composition for each school governing body, varying with the number of pupils on its roll. It did not, in fact, make fundamental changes for voluntary-aided (mainly church) schools beyond the 1980 provisions, since it was still accepted that they should have a working majority of the interests which founded the school originally. Thus aided schools were to have two parent governors (one elected, one a member of the foundation group) and one or two teacher governors. They were also to have a representative of the LEA.

County and controlled schools, on the other hand, were to have between two and five parent governors, varying with the size of school, between two and five LEA governors and in county schools between three and six co-opted governors representing the local community and chosen by the rest. In voluntary-controlled schools the co-opted element was smaller since they also had to have representatives of the foundation sharing this section.

Primary schools were to have a representative of the minor authority, if any, and all schools were to have regard to the desirability of having some representation of business. Head teachers were given an option to be governors or not, but in either case had a right to attend meetings. Grant-maintained schools (covered in later legislation) have between three and five parent governors, one or two teacher governors, the head and enough co-opted 'first' governors (foundation governors in an ex-voluntary-aided school) to give a majority over all other interests. A significant difference is that co-opted governors in LEA schools cannot vote on future co-options, but there is no restriction in grant-maintained schools.

Most schools since 1980 have had to have their own separate governing bodies (thus ending a much abused option before that) but two primary schools serving the same catchment area can share. Wider groupings can sometimes be established with the permission of the Secretary of State.

Parent and teacher governors are elected by secret ballot from parents of pupils at the school and serving teachers at the school respectively. The LEA and foundation (in voluntary schools) appoint their own representatives, and co-opted governors, where appropriate, are chosen by the rest. All governors serve a four-year term from appointment, except teacher governors who cease to be governors if they leave the school. Parent governors may finish their term if they wish even after their child has left.

Governors are in defined circumstances disqualified by a criminal conviction or bankruptcy, or by failing to attend meetings without the governing body's permission for six months. It is extremely difficult, verging on the impossible, to remove a governor from office, especially elected or co-opted governors. Appointed governors may be removed by the appointing body but, according to various court decisions, only in very exceptional circumstances.

Should the head elect to be a governor?

I have chosen not to be a voting governor. With the head's automatic right to attend meetings and to advise and guide governors I am not sure what I would gain, and I fear I would lose a great deal. First, I think it would detract from my status as an independent professional adviser and I would lose my detachment from the rough and tumble of governors' arguments. Second, I should feel undermined if I were outvoted on a matter of great professional importance, and would sooner be instructed to do something I regarded as foolish if that had to be. However, I am picking up that my governors are not happy with my decision and consider me an oddity. Could you advise?

More heads are choosing to be governors, so though you are not an oddity you may be getting just a little more unusual. On your first point, I think we all regard our heads as independent professional advisers whether or not they are governors. I don't think it is an either/or issue. As for the 'rough and tumble' of governors' arguments, that is the process by which many important decisions about the school are legally made.

If you had a difference of opinion with your governors on a matter of major importance I think it would be serious even if you were not a governor. If you were a governor you could fight your corner with less inhibition. Indeed I must go further and say that many heads who choose not to be governors in my experience may try to have it both ways. Strictly speaking if you are not a governor you should limit your contributions to matters of fact and professional practice. You should not attempt to influence decisions on controversial matters by coming down on one side or another. I doubt if there are many non-governor heads who fully accept this position or observe the distinction. It is indeed asking a great deal of them. Heads I know well who are governors value the opportunity to shed the cloak of detachment when, for instance alternative co-optees are being suggested or discussed, when grant-maintained status is under discussion or when the school faces some challenge or danger. They may even value their vote in such cases. As a governor I would have a good feeling about my head being a governor, because I would see it as a willing acceptance of our role and a commitment to our work. But no doubt many who choose the other option have that acceptance and commitment too. The law gives you a choice and you must follow your instinct.

Finding willing LEA governors

You often answer queries about governors representing the LEA who perhaps have too many commitments and are poor attenders and contributors. Our problem is that we have two LEA vacancies out of four unfilled in our school and we understand it is because the LEA can't persuade people to take it on. It has been like this for six months and many schools in the county are the same. Surely even uninterested governors are better than none?

I don't think uninterested governors are better than none. Those who are only there to fill places demoralize and demotivate others. Your LEA must be taking too narrow a view of the kind of person who can represent them. The rest of your letter suggests that there is no problem about finding parent and co-opted governors in your area, so your council must be determined to appoint only party nominees. In many areas LEAs are now quite happy to appoint interested local people with no party label. My own LEA is one, and it advertises for volunteers. Councillors are not obliged to serve, and if they do it is because the school is in their ward and/or they have a family connection. Schools can also put forward candidates. Suggest to your LEA that they cast their net more widely. If the request comes from the whole governing body or, better still, a cluster of governing bodies or, best of all, a local association of governors, it will carry more weight.

Lack of recruits allows dangerous minorities in

I am a head in a poor community with a varied ethnic mix where it is very difficult to get people to offer themselves as governors. I see this situation as dangerous, since 'nature abhors a vacuum' and there is a chance for people who are seeking power or following some private agenda to step in.

Indeed. If enough ordinary people don't come forward to accept the responsibility they have been offered it won't lie idle: it will find its way somewhere less desirable – to central government; back to the local political parties; to heads; or as you fear to unrepresentative people with private agendas. I am afraid there is not any magic answer, since the only safeguard is the vigilant participation of large numbers, and I know that is hard work – especially for the head. We must be thinking about recruiting governors all the time, not just when there are vacancies, making sure the governing body we have is an attraction in terms of the relevance and visibility of its work, that the school communicates well and sensitively with all its constituencies, and that we give people the right messages, particularly that it is their ordinariness we want.

I am bound to say that I spoke at a governors' conference in the area where your school is, and it attracted a huge number of participants whose enthusiasm and commitment, given their obvious 'ordinariness' (a compliment in my vocabulary), I found very moving. One does come across schools with apparently similar catchment areas which have very different levels of public participation. It is worth asking why. I would also urge all who use the phrases 'private agenda' or 'power-seeking' to give those phrases a shake out and dust down from time to time just to make sure they have got the diagnosis right. I know exactly what you mean and fear it too – such people do exist – but often the phrases are a way of dismissing people who are not easy to work with or have challenging views. A few of those can be quite good to have around.

A persistent non-attender

 We have two governors who have disqualified themselves for non-attendance and then been re-appointed by the LEA. They still carry on as before. Is this legal? What can we do?

 I am afraid it is legal. You can as a governing body express your disapproval of colleagues who don't pull their weight and perhaps shame them into better ways. You can also ask your LEA not to do it and point out that it doesn't do their image any good. They don't have to take notice but if we all spoke up we could change things in time.

Problems with appointed governors

We actually have long-standing vacancies for two LEA governors and the three we have are poor attenders. They are governors of other schools and sometimes we wonder if they know which one they are in. It causes a lot of resentment with all the work governors have to do now. Is there no solution?

* * * *

In this voluntary-aided school we have seven members appointed by the Parochial Church Council. Nothing wrong with this, it is a church school and we all support that. But all the foundation governors are men, they are mostly elderly, and really often seem out of touch with modern primary schools and young children. Not only that, but they have done things a certain way for so long that they find it very hard to adapt to the new style of school governing we hope we are moving to, and it is not always easy to make progress. I feel sorry for the head too – she is very dedicated, and go-ahead as well, and I don't always feel she gets the response she deserves.

I get so many letters like this that I feel we should be taking more seriously the question of appointed governors, LEA or foundation – getting enough of them in the first place, and making sure that those we get have time and interest. The LEA and the foundation respectively may appoint whom they wish, but it is quite reasonable for other governors and indeed heads to make representations if there are problems.

In time I hope more LEAs will decide to trawl more widely for LEA governors and not worry too much about their politics. Some have already abandoned the political aspect and advertise for interested and suitable local people. The churches' appointing bodies also vary widely in their policies, some are like yours, but many more use their places for lively young people from the church community, including perhaps some more parents in addition to the one they are legally obliged to include. Please tell the appropriate people what you have told me and encourage other governors you know to do the same.

Why don't church schools have more parent governors?

 I have just been elected as a parent governor to a Church of England primary school. I was amazed to find there was only one place for parents: my friend is a parent governor in a non-church school about the same size and she is one of three. Surely the new system was intended to give all parents more say?

 It was indeed. In county and controlled schools the number of elected parents varies from two to five, depending on the size of the school. Remember, however, that in church schools one of the foundation governors must be a parent, in addition to the elected one, and there is no reason why the church should not choose more parents to represent the foundation interest if they wish.

To understand the difference you must go back a long way to the beginnings of popular education when the churches were the only providers of schools on a significant scale and paid all the costs themselves, but with some help from public funds after 1833. In the public Education Acts of 1870, 1902 and 1944 the church schools were gradually integrated into the growing system of state education, but with important differences which recognized their character and history. If they could not afford to maintain the buildings they became controlled schools (almost indistinguishable from county schools except in religious education, which was in accordance with their own faith). The rest became voluntary-aided schools, with important differences in finance and management. General school subjects are taught in the same way and they observe the national curriculum and all the rules and regulations, they are open to inspection, they may not charge for admission and their governors have very similar powers. In recognition of their continuing financial responsibility for outside maintenance and their denominational needs, however, they retain more control. The law provides for an absolute majority (two or three, depending on the size of the governing body) over all other interests. Thus with the head, an elected parent, one or two elected teachers and a representative of the LEA, you would have seven members appointed by the foundation. Aided schools also retain responsibility for admissions and may give priority to children of their own faith. In fact there is no legal reason why the parent and teacher members should not be increased, but the foundation group would have to be so enlarged to keep the proportion that the governing body would be very big, and I don't know any schools which have done it.

Would-be co-optees waiting outside

 When we have new co-options on the agenda, it all seems a bit cut-and-dried, especially as the people proposed come to the school and wait outside till we have made the decisions. What do you think of this?

 I don't like it. It is intimidating to those making the decision, and looks cut-and-dried even if it is not. It is also an unnecessary embarrassment. Governors should be seen to be making a free choice and if possible should have a number to choose from. I think a little formality does no harm in something so important, and that co-optees should wait until they get an official invitation before putting in an appearance.

I would make an exception of course for those who are already governors and have completed their term, who wish to offer themselves again and who may be at the meeting. They should withdraw for this item, of course. Even this is not ideal, and you could make it the last item so that they can go early.

Can a teacher be co-opted?

 Can a teacher be co-opted as a governor in the school where he teaches? I believe I have something to offer from my activities in the community, quite distinct from my role as a teacher, but I have some idea that teachers have recently been barred from serving except as teacher governors.

 There is no prohibition in LEA schools on co-opting a teacher either in the school where he/she teaches or another, if governors as a body want to do so and can do so within their prescribed number of co-optees. The government did plan some restrictions on teachers serving in any other capacity in schools other than their own a few years ago, but these were dropped. There are some restrictions, however, in grant-maintained schools (see pages 38 and 39).

Non-teaching staff governors

Do you think it advisable to co-opt a member of the non-teaching staff to the governing body, and is it legal?

It is certainly legal. I personally think that the perspective offered by a member of the non-teaching staff is very valuable. It is of course for the whole governing body to decide how it wants to use its limited number of co-options, and there may be strongly competing claims from interests in the community to be considered.

If you do not decide to co-opt, you can always invite a member of the non-teaching staff (or all in turn, or selected ones for agenda items of particular concern to them) to attend as observers, but they would then have no vote.

Governors representing community users

Our school is now extensively used for community activities, and we have a committee to deal with lettings and associated matters. We would like to co-opt at least one representative of our major users to this committee. Are we allowed to do so?

Yes, committees may legally co-opt as many members as governors wish. Normally such members cannot vote, but in the case of a committee concerned with out-of-school use of premises, you will be pleased to hear that a change in the regulations some time ago allows representatives of users to be co-opted exceptionally as full voting members.

Too many teachers?

We have five teachers on our governing body apart from the head. Two are properly elected teacher governors, one parent governor is also a teacher at the school and one co-opted governor is a teacher at another school. I was amazed when we had a vacancy this term that our head suggested we co-opt her deputy, and this was agreed, making the five. We need the professional point of view but is this not a bit excessive? Is it all legal?

Yes, it is all legal in an LEA school if the co-options were properly considered and consciously agreed by a quorate governors' meeting (remember that co-options need a two-thirds quorum of those eligible to vote, and existing co-opted governors can't vote for future co-options). The Secretary of State tried hard a few years ago to restrict the freedom of teachers to serve as governors in other capacities but the proposal went down very badly with many people and was dropped.

I would not myself wish to restrict teachers' rights to be governors or the choice of those who might wish to vote for a teacher or co-opt one. I believe that a proper balance on a governing body is best left to the good sense of the people on the spot. Incidentally even if the Secretary of State's proposals had gone through, they would not have forbidden teachers to be governors in another capacity *in their own schools*, because this right is safeguarded in the 1986 Act.

I would not generalize about how much teacher representation is 'excessive'. It depends on how they behave and how they see their role; on the strength of the other governors; and on the relationships between head and staff. In general I think governing bodies benefit from a little more teacher input than the law provides, and that most people have the sense to realize that if they represent parents or the LEA or the wider community that must be the main perspective which they bring to the governing body even if they are also teachers. I should only be concerned if, in a school where the head tended to be very territorial, she seemed to be trying to surround herself with supportive and compliant governors, and with deputies this is often a danger to watch for.

Unless a deputy has been freely elected by the staff to represent them, I think it could be preferable for him/her to attend as an observer. But even this, never mind the much bigger step of co-opting the deputy, is for governors as a whole to approve, and remember that every one of us has some responsibility for what happens.

Too cosy

I find that unless you are very careful a head can easily create a governing body on which most members are in some way dependent on his or her goodwill. Obvious examples are deputies as teacher governors, teachers as parent governors and support staff co-opted. This is not too bad unless you then find that other governors get jobs as midday supervisors, cleaners or classroom assistants. In this inner city in the North of England where unemployment is really high people are grateful for the work and won't easily speak out of turn. What chance is there of an independent voice?

I don't think there are heads who would deliberately set out to pack the governing body with compliant people, though the sub-conscious pull to a quieter life can be quite strong and we *all* need to watch that we don't shy away from a good but challenging choice when we have the option of someone more harmonious on our various interest groups. Don't forget, however, that it takes two to tango, and some of the moves you describe are within governors' control. We do have legal responsibility for all appointments and we decide on co-options. As for teachers standing as parent governors and deputies being elected teacher governors, the natural outcome of a governing body known to be too cosy would be a reaction in time of parents and teachers against more of the same, and they would act to restore some balance when there is next a vacancy. I agree that governors need to be vigilant and use what scope they have to bring in more independent voices. But we cannot regulate everything.

A husband and wife on the same board

Is it legal for a husband and wife to be on the same governing body?

Yes, I know of no reason why they should not, provided they have got there by regular means which are above board and not unfairly influenced. I have heard many governors say they don't think it proper, but I don't think it would bother me. After all there are all sorts of close relationships, and not all of them open either. Being on a governing body requires all members to be independent in their thinking and professional in their detachment. We all as governors have to cope with many relationships which in such an essentially intimate community test our ability to put feelings aside, and marriage is only one. Sometimes, as with co-options, governors will have a chance to resist such an appointment if it upsets them, but if it is an elected or appointed governor they may not be able to do anything about it.

Party politics still dominate co-options and elections

 We still have a very heavy political influence on co-options, with appointed LEA governors bringing forward names when there is a vacancy. We could easily go back to the days when a majority of governors were of one political persuasion, since even some parent elections have a political element. How can we avoid this?

 It is in your hands as far as co-options are concerned. The more you fall into the trap, the more you risk what you fear. Remember that co-opted governors can't vote on new co-options. The main danger is being unprepared. You should anticipate vacancies, which rarely arise suddenly, and be ready with alternative nominations of people (get their permission first of course) who can be shown to have something to offer or a track record of interest in the school. A school should in any case be looking for new recruits all the time, so as not to be caught unprepared when there is a vacancy. Try to interest your head in this question too because he/she is in a good position to work for a better balance. Often in areas where one party has been in power a long time, heads either regard it as normal that there should be this sort of manipulation or see the political party as some kind of protector. With the new independence of schools this is an out-of-date attitude.

'First' governors in a grant-maintained school

   Is it right that co-opted governors are in a majority in a grant-maintained school? If so how can the governing body prevent domination at some future time by a faction of some kind?

   Your assumption is correct. The 'first' governors (foundation governors in a voluntary-aided school) must outnumber the other governors (who include elected parents and teachers and the head teacher). Your second question raises an issue which concerns many people in relation to GMS and I would personally agree that there are risks in having a majority drawn from outside the school which call for a great deal of vigilance by other governors. The danger is greater in as much as existing governors may vote in future co-options which is not the case in LEA schools. The Act provides, however, that two of the first governors must be parents of registered pupils and that those appointing first governors must be satisfied that they are members of the local community 'committed to the good government and continuing viability of the school'. They must also ensure representation of business.

Teachers' right to be governors in grant-maintained schools

   Can you tell me please whether there is any restriction on teachers serving as parent, foundation or first governors in grant-maintained schools? I cannot find anything in writing about it but someone told me it was so. I know the government tried to bring in this restriction in LEA schools and dropped it because of the strong opposition. Is this a back door?

   Section 3 of Schedule 5 to the 1993 Education Act prohibits the appointment of any member of the staff of a grant-maintained school as a first governor of that school. There are no restrictions on teachers holding other governorships, e.g. as parent governors, or any governorships (even first governors) in schools other than their own. Finally, there are no restrictions of any kind on teachers holding governorships in county or voluntary schools, even those in which they teach. As you say the government dropped their plan to restrict teachers' rights more generally. I don't think one can read too much into the position in grant-maintained schools. We know already that the government is not keen on too many teachers being governors, but grant-maintained schools are different in many significant ways, not least in that first governors are in the majority, so the influence of teachers could perhaps as the government sees it be undesirably extended by that route.

Should I continue as a governor when my last child leaves?

 My second child leaves this school in July and I then complete my four-year-term anyway. I have been a keen and committed parent governor, and although it took me a while to dare open my mouth, and a bit longer to be confident in my contribution, I do feel that now I am a useful member of the board. I am sure I could get myself co-opted if I made a bid for it, but is this fair? I have done my share of griping about 'dead wood', of which we have some prime examples, and I feel strongly that schools need active governors and new blood. Should I make way for someone new? Would I be hypocritical to stay when I have wished others would move on?

 You don't sound a bit like dead wood to me. Indeed the very fact that you have enough stirrings of conscience to raise the matter puts you in a different class from the governors who don't even begin to realize the commitment needed. You *will* be making way for someone new in the shape of a new parent governor anyway. Don't deprive the governing body of your hard-won capability just yet. Have you considered whether there is a particular bit of dead wood you could replace, thus performing a double service? Look at the period of service of your fellow governors to see who will be coming to the end at the same time as you or soon after. If there is a co-opted governor who could qualify for well-earned retirement, that is convenient, and you then need to ensure that you get someone to nominate you and prepare the ground before a *fait accompli* takes place. However, it may be that your dead wood is in the LEA group, and that your co-opted governors are active. If this is so, consider whether there is any chance of your getting in there instead. Many LEAs are now giving up the political connection and are happy to consider people of proven usefulness to fill at least some of their seats, especially since the number of governorships anyone can hold was reduced to two. If it seems promising and the timing is right you could be performing a real service. But be sure not to lose both chances.

Can we vote to remove our chairman?

 Our chairman has grossly abused his position as a governor by being disloyal to a decision made by the majority. I know about the procedures for voting him out of the chair but that doesn't help much because we shall certainly not re-elect him anyway. We actually want to vote him off the governing body. Can we do this?

 There is no procedure for voting a colleague off the governing body. The most you can do is a vote of censure and a request for resignation, but it is his decision. I agree that this is a particularly grave misdemeanour, but it is impossible to remove elected or co-opted governors for anything other than bankruptcy, criminal offences or six months non-attendance. Appointed governors (i.e. foundation or LEA) can be removed by the appointing body, but case-law indicates that this is only in certain restricted circumstances. It has been agreed in these legal cases that they can be removed if they have ceased to represent the LEA (e.g. after a change of control in an election). They cannot be removed for not following the policies of the appointing body when the action or decision complained of is within governors' powers. It is possible that an appointed governor might be legally removed by the appointing body (not by the other governors) for action which is ultra vires, but this has not been legally tested as far as I know.

Can we resign as a body?

 We have a simple question. We governors as a body are opposed to seeking grant-maintained status. It is not a party political matter, but to do with our relationships in a fairly small LEA and our feeling that we are part of one service. If our parents vote for GM status, and we immediately resign as a body, who would replace us? We could not be re-formed under GM rules until the application was approved, and the

LEA (which though Conservative does not support this particular policy) would surely have no interest in reconstituting the governing body under the normal rules simply so that it could apply for GM status?

 Technically you would not resign 'as a body' but as nine, twelve or sixteen individuals, all feeling that they did not want to be associated with a grant-maintained school. The LEA in this situation has no alternative but to replace you under normal rules as quickly as possible. Until any application to the Secretary of State is approved, you remain a county school for which the LEA is responsible, and part of that responsibility is to ensure that you have a governing body to carry out its duties, including that of putting in the application for GM status if necessary.

We must always bear in mind that it is parents who make the decision however we feel as governors. Our only role is to decide for or against holding a ballot, and even in this some would argue that if we had evidence that a significant number of parents wanted it we should not ignore that: they can in any case activate it without us on a 20% petition as you know. Too much vocal governor opposition in these circumstances might be counter-productive and rob you of your important role of ensuring a balanced debate.

I should not myself feel that it was right (as distinct from legal) to resign between ballot and the granting of GM status. It is in a way flouting the parents' legal decision, which it becomes your duty to see through the various processes. Furthermore, there is always the chance that the application could be refused, in which case the school could do without a gratuitous upheaval in its governing body as it begins the process of readjustment. The time to consider your position is when the application has been approved. That I agree is very difficult for any governor who has opposed it. On the one hand, you will want to ensure that the school keeps its character, remains responsive to its community, and maintains policies which you consider equitable. You will also want to see it through a difficult transition and try to get everybody pulling together again. On the other hand you may feel that it cannot be the school to which you first volunteered your service, however hard you try, and that your opposition is such as to render you a less than effective governor, better replaced by someone with commitment to the new order.

Do we have to share a governing body?

 Our primary school shares a governing body with another on the same site. I understand the law allows this, but are we obliged to accept it? It is getting increasingly difficult to give proper consideration to school-specific matters, e.g. budget issues.

 The 1986 Act allows LEAs if they wish to establish shared governing bodies for two primary schools serving the same catchment area without special permission. Other groupings require the Secretary of State's consent. I agree with you that it is unsatisfactory and is becoming more so as the volume of business increases and the kind of issues governors have to deal with more sensitive. The Taylor Committee's report, on which the 1986 Act was largely based, recommmended no grouping. My postbag suggests that, while the occasional school sees positive advantages, most do not like it. Indeed, if all those who did not like it wrote to their MPs that would amount to a lot of letters. You should at least make clear to your LEA that you would like separate bodies. Some don't use the grouping option at all, and all ought to take their schools' wishes into account.

Grouped governing bodies in Wales

 I thought individuals were only allowed to be governors of two schools. In this Welsh county nearly all primary schools are grouped and many are in groups of three and I think even four in some cases with special permission from the Welsh Office. The LEA appointees on these combined boards could be governors of six or more schools. Surely this is not legal. They haven't the time, and loyalties are divided.

 I am afraid it is legal, though like you I don't think it is desirable. What the law says is that an individual may not be on more than two *governing bodies*. This does allow the sort of situation you describe. I have heard it said indeed that grouping is favoured in some places because it allows the available supply of party nominees to be involved in the maximum number of schools. Many schools don't seem to like sharing governing bodies, and the only thing they can do is keep saying so to their LEA, to MPs and to their Secretary of State (for Wales in your case).

Governors' term of office

At our annual parents' meeting two points were strongly made about governors' period of office.

First, it was thought that a parent governor whose child left a year ago should not continue, but he is not intending to resign. Is he within his rights to stay?

Second, parents were worried about continuity. In a year's time we will only have four members out of eighteen still within their term. Parents thought a percentage of governors should be asked to resign each year so we always have a nucleus of experienced people. The chairman said this was illegal.

A parent governor's period of office is legally four years, the same as other governors. It is not open to a school to change these rules. Before 1986 parent governors had to resign when their children left, and the reasons for changing the rule were, I understand, to provide equality of treatment for parent governors with LEA and co-opted ones; to allow parent governors to put their hard-won experience to good use; and to give more status to parent governors by allowing them time to demonstrate their effectiveness. I support these reasons for change. If the choice is between more direct representation and more effective representation I think parents' interests gain more strength and status from the latter. Any governor can resign before completing the full term: parent governors will vary in their attitude to this. Some will be grateful for the chance to put their experience to good use a bit longer, others will feel that they are getting out of touch and that their interest is transferring to the next stage of education with their child. Some may even sense that they are not seen to be representative any more, and most would be sensitive to any suggestion that parents wanted a change.

Your parents' suggestion about rolling representation is also out of line with the law, except to the extent that it happens naturally or through individuals choosing to leave earlier of their own volition. In fact the system will in time provide its own rolling effect: before the 1986 Act a governing body was dissolved en masse after local elections, but the four-year-period of office means that as the cumulative total of mid-term changes mounts up, a typical governing body will have a good deal of carry-over. Remember too that there is no reason why governors in any category should not offer themselves again, and a governing body concerned about continuity will encourage good colleagues to do so, urge LEAs and foundations to re-appoint some, and co-opt good people again.

The one aspect of turnover which bothers me is that, where a governing body has had a big change, as yours will, there may not for some weeks be enough people to get on with the co-options: co-options need a two-thirds quorum and existing co-optees may not vote. This leaves only a small number to elect a chair.

Parent governors and the PTA

A parent governor was elected to a casual vacancy last term who has never taken part in any PTA activity, much less put herself forward for the committee. Committee members, including our hard-working secretary, were also candidates but she beat them with a very large vote. It seems very unfair to all those who work hard for the school, and we can only think that she won support by promising parents privately that she would work to change various things about the school that they don't like. Can any action be taken against people who get voted in on false promises?

There would be plenty of politicians in trouble if false promises became a sacking matter. As in any other democratic process people are often taken at their face value, and only time and the pressures of those who elect them can bring their credibility into question. I can't help wondering what lies behind all this. The parent must have some strong appeal to get such a large vote, and if she is so keen, what is she doing outside the PTA? The suggestion that there are things about the school that many parents don't like also raises the question of what the PTA is doing to improve communication with parents and air their concerns. Perhaps your PTA committee should at least ask themselves whether the PTA has a cliquey reputation, whether there is any significant body of parents who don't feel included, and whether they carry 'working hard for the school' to the point of blindly supporting every single thing it does. I could be quite wrong: maybe your new governor is just someone who does not find organizing fund-raising or social events very appealing but has some ideas about what a parent governor might do. But I always regard a clear anti-PTA vote in a parent governor election as a possible danger sign.

Can a teacher become a parent governor in her own school?

 A teacher in our school who stood unsuccessfully for teacher governor has now proposed herself as a parent governor to fill a casual vacancy. She has her two children here. Surely this is not allowed?

 It is legal. The 1986 Act specifically allows the candidature in one category of a person eligible to stand in another category in that school. Even if the government had been successful a few years ago in preventing teachers standing as parent, LEA or co-opted governors in *other* schools (a proposal which caused such an outcry that it was dropped) they would have been unable to do anything about the issue in the teacher's own school without an amendment to the legislation. But teachers in grant-maintained schools may not be co-opted as first governors of their own schools.

While I totally support teachers' right to stand as parent governors in general - and argued the case strongly when it was in question - I think it may be a difficult task for them to be parent governors in the school where they teach. There could be conflicts of loyalty, but that is a matter for them and those who elect them. If parents are not easy with it they won't do it. I should certainly not wish the right to be taken away, since it is an interference both with the parental rights of the teacher and the freedom of other parents to choose whom they wish. After all we all have to balance loyalties sometimes.

A governor who has removed her child to a private school

 In our area there are many independent prep schools and our five–to– eleven school loses a number of pupils at seven. Our budget suffers. One of our parent governors has just removed her child to an independent school, though she says she is very satisfied with the education we have provided and is otherwise supportive. Can we request her resignation? And can I as head make it clear when we re-elect parent governors that candidates should be committed to keeping their children with us from five to eleven?

 I understand your point of view, and in the similar area where I live many governors feel as strongly as you. But although there is no reason why governors should not make their disapproval of colleagues clear if they wish, no-one can *compel* an elected governor to resign. Nor could you legally insist on the kind of undertaking you suggest from prospective governors. Indeed, while understanding how you feel, I should not approve of any action which restricted parents' free choice. I would agree that governors have a public role and anything seen as less than total confidence in the school can be damaging. I have seen a local governor 'culture' develop which unmistakably expresses such feelings. But I think we must stop short of appearing to dictate people's family choices or start witch-hunts.

Business governors in a voluntary controlled school

 As a voluntary-controlled school with 200+ pupils we have no co-opted governors (the one place which would have been for a co-optee goes to the minor authority) and no scope for importing particular skills. What do we do about business interests? And can we decide to co-opt an additional governor over and above the categories provided for (LEA and minor authority, foundation, parent, teacher) someone with, say, financial expertise or some experience of fund-raising?

 The business interest requirement can be met from any group, not just co-optees. Unless your parents happen to elect someone with a business background it is up to the appointing groups (foundation, LEA, minor authority) to get together and decide that one of them will propose a suitable person. After all you have three foundation and three LEA nominees. Similarly, if a group of present governors knows anyone with the experience they are looking for, they are free to request that the LEA appoints that person to their next vacancy, or the foundation if it is someone involved in the church. They are not obliged to accept your suggestion, but often appointing bodies welcome ideas. You may not increase the total size of your governing body beyond what the law prescribes, but there is no reason why you should not invite non-voting visitors with the experience you need.

Can a governor be removed?

I am one of those parent governors who finds it hard to get the facilities to communicate with other parents. Any suggestion that I have tried to find out what parents I meet think about some issue, or that some of them have approached me, causes the chairman's wrath to descend on me. He says it is not my role, that there is nothing special about a parent governor – well I am sure you know all about that. Now, in the worst outburst yet, he says he is going to get me off the governing body, which the LEA can do, because of my persistent refusal to toe the line.

What a bully. I can assure you that in no circumstances can the LEA dismiss a parent governor or a teacher or co-opted governor. They can in extreme cases withdraw the powers of the *whole* governing body if it has grossly mismanaged the school. Only in very rare cases can even an LEA governor be dismissed: there have been a few cases in the courts, and even though the 1986 Act says the LEA may dismiss anyone they have appointed, the case-law suggests that this only applies if the person has become totally unrepresentative as a result of a change in party control. LEA governors certainly cannot be dismissed for not voting in accordance with the LEA's policies. If you were to upset a number of your fellow governors they could record a vote of censure or even call on you to resign, but it would be your decision.

Recruitment and induction

 Can you give any guidance on better recruitment and induction?

The best recruiting agency is a governing body whose work is real, relevant and visible in the school. People will want to join it if it presents a good image in these respects. If they think it is irrelevant to the education of children they will take some persuasion to leave their comfort and their hobbies. Visibility is also important and no effort should be spared to inform parents and teachers of the work and concerns of the governing body.

Parents will be easier to recruit in a school which informs and consults them, makes them feel not just welcome but needed, and helps existing parent governors to communicate with and represent them. Teacher governors similarly will be keen to serve if the role is seen as real and important, and in particular if they are encouraged to contribute and participate freely and represent their colleagues without fear. Some of the poor practice reported in these columns, demonstrating how badly some governing bodies look after individuals in difficulty, would be sure to turn recruits away or guarantee that places will be filled by harmless but ineffective ones.

As far as co-opted governors are concerned, schools should be recruiting all the time, not just when vacancies occur. This is not just a matter of how well the school and its governors present themselves, but also of how energetically they trawl for suitable people. Think carefully about groups who ought to be better represented and how to access them – tenants' and residents' associations, community groups, ethnic minorities, other agencies concerned with children, feeder and follow-on institutions, as well as business interests. If the LEA or your foundation are appointing people who don't contribute much, have not got the time, or are not in touch with modern education, tackle that head-on and point out how it lets the side down. Suggest people yourselves.

As for induction of new members, we are usually appalling, quite uncivilized, in the way we welcome newcomers to anything. We let them pick up the names, roles and jargon as they go along, mumble, tell in-jokes, and never find out what people have to offer till it is too late.

It is not even difficult when one thinks about it. It just needs planning. The head should contact new governors at once, inviting them to the school to welcome them, giving them a staff list with responsibilities, a plan of the building, a list of events, and a warm invitation to come in soon to look at something specific. The chair should contact them too, explaining a little about the main current issues. The outgoing governor should contribute a well-weeded file, and another governor should be delegated to invite them for a cup of tea, lend a helpful book, offer to go with them to the first meeting or to a training session. Then the meeting should be preceded by a little social time, and when it starts members should introduce themselves properly and everybody give some indication of their interests and experience. Remember it extends the floundering stage by months if you don't have any kind of opening to a conversation with a colleague or don't even know if they are councillors or teachers. The new member should be brought quickly into some not-too-daunting activity, and if you talk at all about skills, remember to be clear that you don't mean word-processing, marketing, accountancy or the law, but listening, peacemaking, organizing. Finally, remember that too much informality can exclude people just as surely as too much formality.

3 The curriculum

This is probably the most difficult responsibility for governors to take hold of, partly because they think they need a lot of knowledge before they can begin, partly because they suspect - with some justification – that many teachers are defensive about intrusion into what used to be called their 'secret garden'.

It stands to reason that a welder, a private secretary, a check-out assistant in a supermarket, a builder, a corn and seed merchant, nurse, motor mechanic or accountant is never going to compete with the kind of knowledge and expertise that a teacher has acquired in four years of study and years of practice. That is not the level at which governors operate at all. We shall learn a great deal, but even then we shall not presume to judge the best way to help children to learn. On the other hand, all governors have some idea of the information and skills young people need when they go out into the world, and most will have a pretty shrewd idea when some part of the learning process is not working properly. They will not know the reasons or the remedies necessarily, but they will know how to find out.

Look at the first question and answer in this section. The governor who makes fan-assisted ovens knows that it is for an engineer to discover why the fans do not last the life of the oven, for an engineer/designer to produce an improved model, and for a works manager to rearrange his schedule to step up production of replacement fans meanwhile. But somewhere a board of directors who are not engineers, designers or works managers will have seen the necessity for these moves and authorized them. They may have to will the means as well as the end in the form of extra capital, extra staff and the temporary postponement of other important activity. They may have to break away from regular practice and authorize free replacement of fans in ovens less than five years old, another decision which has its price. These are management decisions and they will have been based on sound management information – sales figures, returns from authorised service agencies, claims under guarantee, complaints.

Governors have their management information too, and they are also in close contact with the school's customers. They can ask questions, commission investigative or remedial activity, monitor progress.

The school you first come into as a governor is working. It has been going for a long time, is not starting from scratch right now. It is a mature garden, not a near-virgin plot. You do not go around digging things up to see if they are growing or changing plants around, especially as you are not a trained horticulturist. But you know they need light, water, plant-food, regular inspection for pests. You can help create the environment in which growth can continue.

In school you will listen carefully and ask questions, making it clear that you only want to learn. You will observe classes at work whenever you can. Meanwhile good management of the budget, wise appointments of staff and concern for their welfare and professional development, care of the building and its amenities, and encouragement of pupil activities and a caring atmosphere, are the means by which governors help to provide the conditions for good learning. Soon you will be collecting little bits of management information about learning itself – from pupils, parents, exam and test results, subjects chosen. Before long heads and teachers will be asking for your opinions, support, consent, help with something. It may be a problem that has arisen. It may be a choice to be made, a change they have considered and think would improve learning, or a development that needs resourcing. You will mostly rely heavily on their professional judgement. But you will be beginning to have some insights and opinions, and sometimes you will have more questions. Good teachers know that passive or uncritical support is not worth having. The process you undertake with the curriculum is agreement with professionals on what you both want to achieve, consent to the methods they propose to use, and a joint effort to assess outcomes.

Governors do not, I repeat, get involved in the way teachers manage learning in the classroom. If there is anything which causes them concern they must find some other way of bringing it into the appropriate arena for governors. If it is something dangerous or illegal – corporal punishment for instance – then the head should be alerted. But if it is to do with how things are taught, organizing ability groups, infringing some important policy like equal opportunities, the governor will have to engineer some information exchange or discussion in which the issues can be explained or explored impersonally by governors as a whole.

Major curriculum changes – a new reading scheme, a subject added to or dropped from the curriculum, a different exam board or syllabus

– should always be presented for governors' approval. It is for professionals to convince us, and it is always up to those who want change to justify it. We may be totally convinced. We may have searching questions to ask. Or we may be able to warn about the likely reception of a change by parents, for whom it may be a bit startling or premature. We can advise caution, and if we are convinced, perhaps help the school to explain and reassure.

There are some aspects of the curriculum which are underlined, as it were, in the responsibilities given to governors in the law. These are religious education and worship, sex education and special needs. They are all subjects which come close to parents and should always be looked at with their feelings in mind.

A business governor grapples with the curriculum

 My company makes fan-assisted ovens. It is a bit remote from Key Stage 3 and double certification science and set books. I just don't know what the role of a governor like myself is. Teachers have had four years' training and perhaps fifteen to twenty years' experience. How can I possibly have anything significant to say to justify my oversight of the curriculum?

 If thousands of fan-assisted ovens were out of service because fans had failed, your board of directors would do two things. Long term they would commission some research on why the fans were not surviving the life of the oven. Short term they would step up the production of fans, perhaps at the expense of their other lines, on the existing model, to ensure supplies. That is a management decision, by people who are not necessarily engineers or designers. Engineers or designers have to research the causes of failure and design improved models, and workplace management organise the increase in production. The board have seen that something is not working and used their general experience to guide the efforts of experts.

You would have a similar situation in a school if, in response to the national curriculum, your staff had decided to adopt a new broad science course and in their professional wisdom had made a choice of exam board and syllabus. They had also, we will imagine, set up new student groupings to allow for the fact that students of all abilities now took science, ordered new textbooks (which because of the demand only arrived in February), and re-assigned staff. The exam results were extremely disappointing.

As governors you could identify certain lines of enquiry. Was it the right course for mixed ability students? Were the ability groupings right? Were the staff sufficiently adjusted to teaching the whole age group, some of whom found science very hard? Or was it all because of the late arrival of textbooks, teething troubles of a new system? Should we be sure not to overreact? You as governors can ask these questions, but experts have to answer them. Perhaps like your directors you would suggest lines of long-term enquiry and meanwhile ensure short term that the new cohort had a textbook each on 7 September, introduce smaller teaching groups at the temporary expense of groups lower down the school, and perhaps look at strengthening the staff of the faculty.

I hope I have made the point that we are there to see whether things are working and use experience from our own world to ask questions which in the end teachers have to answer.

After all you would raise your eyebrows at least if the school proposed to drop French in favour of Norwegian. Nothing wrong with Norwegian, but parents might not see it as the language of international commerce and discourse. You might be the sort of governor who would think it very wrong to allow music, art, drama to be dropped wholesale by student choice after fourteen just because the compulsory curriculum had been slimmed down to English, maths and science. You probably have views about whether statistics is more use than Latin, media studies than sociology, history than home economics. These are decisions governors will have to contribute to now that time has been released for schools to make their own choices. It is not necessary for us to know how to conduct a laboratory experiment – or why the fans had such a short life – but we make the framework within which questions can be answered.

Have governors a right to discuss a new reading scheme?

 This primary school is proposing to drop the graded readers used for thirty years or more, and a number of new schemes and combinations of schemes are under discussion. Governors have not been involved, but we know there will be a lot of trouble with more old-fashioned parents. Is it within our responsibilities?

 Policy on the teaching of reading is in my view central and part of governors' responsibility for strategic curriculum decisions. Of course we need teachers to argue the pros and cons of the options and convince us that what they propose is right. But it is folly for professionals to embark on something so emotive for many parents without taking governors with them.

Considering the options

Can we set up a small group to consider a proposal to change the options system? The alternatives (there are several) proposed by the school's policy committee, are quite radical, so the head, properly in our view, wants governors' agreement.

You can establish a working party to do the spade-work and set out the issues for governors. But curriculum decisions can't be delegated – the whole governing body must make them.

A governors' curriculum study group

We have an excellent curriculum study group – we were careful not to call it a committee – which looks at every department's work in turn with full teacher co-operation. We pull out the key issues on such things as options, sex education and choices of exam board, and report to the full governors, and we do the first analysis of the exam results to guide governors. We keep a constant watch on special needs, keep the arts in the limelight, advise on issues which need careful PR with parents and warn about any changes which parents may not easily accept. We think we are really useful! Now we have a new head who says governors should not concern themselves with the detail of the curriculum and teachers should not engage independently in this sort of discussion with governors. It would greatly help us if you could confirm that what we are doing is good practice.

I think the practice you describe is excellent. It greatly improves understanding between governors and staff to talk about the school's work in a relaxed small group, and your reports will represent a significant resource for governors and improve the quality of their debate. Should you ever have a problem with any aspect of the school's work, you will have a good base of knowledge and can tackle it without appearing threatening.

I can assure your head that many schools follow this good practice. Governors have responsibility for the effectiveness of the school's learning programme so must keep themselves informed of what is going on, and I am sure you don't get involved in excessive detail. It is quite proper for teachers to be involved in working parties of this kind, and in my experience they have welcomed the interest of governors and the chance to describe their work to them.

You must realize that new heads often feel apprehensive about the kind of set-up they are inheriting and perhaps it could be threatening to come to a governing body so heavily involved and well-organized, especially if this contrasts with what previous experience they have had – which often is not much. There is a natural tendency when newly appointed to want to 'take hold of things'. Turn the wick down just a bit to allow for this and lose no opportunity to assure your head of your goodwill and support and your lack of any ambition to run the school. Show him your papers, suggest he talks to some of the teachers who have worked with you if he is nervous about their involvement, and of course make him welcome to attend. I hope it will be possible to resolve this on a basis of reassurance and growth of trust, but in the last resort of course it is not the head's decision. Governing bodies decide what committees and working parties they set up and how they organize their work generally.

Why all this topic work?

  As a new primary school governor I am of course taking an interest in what the children are learning, and like many others I judge it I suppose from when I was in school. I can't complain about the thoroughness of the number work or the huge efforts made to produce fluent readers, but an awful lot of time is spent on 'topics' which seem like glorified scrap books with cuttings and drawings. In one case I saw bus timetables and a 'pop-up' model of a rickshaw, even in the junior department. I wish I knew what the children get out of all this. I don't dare say anything for fear of being labelled an interfering old has-been.

  If you had been a school governor in the 1960s you might well have found that the primary school was dominated by topic work and that a lot of the teachers would get very irate if anyone questioned it. You may have found mistakes uncorrected, creative writing bursting out all over with no thought for spelling or grammar, reading apparently taught by guesswork and any sort of free painting praised to the skies. At least that was how innocent outsiders saw it, though there was much exciting work going on and the number of schools where it was all unstructured was probably very small indeed.

Now there has been a reaction and most primary schools are a bit more structured with considerable emphasis on basic skills – you have noticed that. 'Free expression' has to justify itself. But much that was good has remained, and among those good things is the practice of following a theme, perhaps for a whole term, like water, transport, homes. The study is carefully planned – I once saw a teacher's plan of the different stages and was amazed by how careful it was and wished all governors could see it – bringing in maths, science, art, history and geography, all in a way which would hold a child's interest. Remember everything now has to meet the attainment targets of the national curriculum, and the work gets covered even if it is not in subject compartments.

Why don't you ask if one of your teachers could come to a governors' meeting and demonstrate the value of topics in terms of learning goals? I am sure it would be an eye-opener.

Our parents can't afford school activities

 One by one out-of-school activities have disappeared from the life of this school in an area of severe deprivation. Parents just cannot afford the voluntary contributions, yet the children here desperately need to have learning come to life for them and to get into more stimulating environments. Before LMS our LEA was generous in its funding for schools such as ours and we were able to accomplish a great deal. It seems that the present funding formula does not allow discrimination in our favour. Yet children in better-off areas also have a lot of outings and other activity organized by their parents. It is not fair.

 I only wish I could say something beyond agreeing that it is not fair. I am just waiting for enough governors to write to MPs and anybody else they can think of to point out the effects of basing so much of a school's budget on numbers alone, and so little on differing needs. Many disadvantaged schools show ingenuity in finding stimulating activities which don't make demands on parents, and also raise or re-schedule funds to make contributions unnecessary, but there are limits to what can be achieved in areas as poor as yours. The only short-term possibilities are sponsorship (try to think of a project which might stir the imagination of a possible sponsor) or local charities. It would make a telling point if the parents of some lucky school were to adopt a less lucky one not too far away and fund some joint out-of-school activity.

The arts in schools

 Just two of us on our governing body feel very concerned about the effect which pressures on time and funds have on creative activity in schools. Our fellow governors understand about supporting pupils who have special musical talent, say, and putting on a good school play or concert. They might also agree that some creative work helps people enjoy their leisure. But they seem unaware that there is any more to teaching the arts in schools than this. We can see the standard of whole-classroom activity in the arts in steady decline. How can we argue convincingly for what we see as a basic entitlement?

 The first thing to say is that music and art are still foundation subjects in the national curriculum up to fourteen, that dance is included specifically in the national curriculum for PE, while drama is dealt with within English. We lost the post-fourteen commitment on music and art and the separate recognition for drama and dance, but there is still a considerable entitlement which governors cannot ignore. Also cultural and aesthetic development have their place in the law and its supportive literature as objectives of education.

People often need only a little help to see that the aims of arts education go far beyond the development of individual talent and leisure enrichment. We can easily show how many transferable skills are involved: inventiveness, planning, teamwork, persistence to get it right, and even direct links with other subjects – history, geography, mathematics. We can emphasize that these are not 'soft-centred' activities but rigorous and demanding. We can suggest that creative subjects help pupils to understand themselves and others, to make sense of experience, to manage relationships better, to work co-operatively, to develop self-esteem. Wiser employers will also value these benefits. We can point out how helpful creative activity is to pupils with learning difficulties or disabilities, and how it helps all young people to deal with anger, frustration and conflict in their own lives. It can spread the experience of success among a much wider range of pupils, and this will benefit other areas of learning.

Try to encourage all your fellow governors to go into school and observe the best it can offer in the teaching of creative subjects. The enthusiasm of a good teacher is infectious, and an hour of observation is worth a week of preaching.

Finally, there is an excellent video pack produced for schools with the help of the Gulbenkian Foundation called *Valuing the Arts* which will help persuade the so-far unpersuaded. Schools can buy it for only £5, including postage, from the Gulbenkian Foundation, 98 Portland Place, London W1. The Foundation also offers a very good book, *The Arts in Schools* for £9.50, including post and packing. Governors may like to know that the Gulbenkian Foundation is keen to support exceptionally imaginative creative arts projects by governors and governor training agencies.

Payment for instrumental teaching

Parents have been expressing concern to me about charges made for instrumental tuition in school, and as a parent governor I must respond. Without explanation they have been told that they will now have to pay for lessons. Is this legal? This is small-group tuition, not individual lessons.

I am afraid the 1993 Education Act changed the position, and since October 1993 it has been legal to charge for instrumental tuition in groups of up to four pupils, not just individual tuition as laid down in the 1988 Act. Charges may be waived for families on income support, no charges are made in respect of pupils being prepared for public examinations, and charges must not exceed the actual cost of the tuition. I realize that these mitigating provisions still don't cover parents' concerns, since there will still be financial strain on families in many cases and pupils can't get as far as entering for public examinations if parents can't afford instrumental lessons at earlier stages.

I am concerned that you as governors were taken by surprise. Governors are responsible within the law for a school's charging policy. Remember the law doesn't lay down precisely what LEAs and schools do: it merely says what you *can't* do (i.e. in general make charges for education) and establishes exceptions to the prohibition. Although the choices available in practice may be limited, it is up to schools to decide in detail how they respond to changes of this kind, and governors should be fully involved in decisions. I do not know whether your PTA raise funds to support activities which attract charges or voluntary contributions, but I know that in many schools they consider it so important that school music or school trips should not be curtailed by inability to pay, that they give priority to these things in fund-raising, even though they may feel strongly as many do that it ought not to be necessary. Some local charities may also support music education in cases of need.

How much sex education?

 I still feel I do not know enough about current provisions on sex education. I understand about secondary schools and the parental right to withdraw pupils there from lessons, but what about primary schools? I am a governor of a middle school (classified as primary): are we not allowed to provide anything further? Most of us on the governing body would think broader sex education than the birds and bees level was necessary for 12-year-olds.

 I agree: much younger than twelve indeed in my own view, and your governing body is right to be concerned. In all types of school national curriculum science – from which there is no right of withdrawal – will include appropriate factual information about the biological aspects of sex for the age group concerned. It is not quite fair to refer to it as birds and bees, though I know this is only shorthand: it will include full information about human reproduction and associated matters, but will not include the social, moral and emotional aspects of sexual relationships or (any longer) about HIV and AIDS. Those aspects will be covered by the sex education programme provided under the governors' own policies, and here there is a clear difference between primary and secondary schools.

In secondary schools additional sex education *must* be provided under governors' policies and it must include information about HIV and AIDS. In primary schools governors still have an obligation to establish a *policy* on sex education and to make it available to parents, but the school is not obliged to provide any sex education outside the national curriculum. In other words the governors' policy could in theory be to have *no* sex education other than what is compulsory, but in practice they have to be prepared to justify that decision to their teachers and parents. I would expect that most primary schools and certainly those with pupils as old as twelve would want to provide a good deal more than they are legally obliged to do –

about the emotional aspects of physical development of boys and girls; about family life and the responsibilities of parenthood; loving and caring relationships; saying no to unwanted attentions; gender equality issues; and so on. Remember that the policy need not necessarily provide for specific 'sex lessons', since much of what needs to be communicated comes into almost every aspect of the primary school's work including literature, history, the environment, health education, projects, and above all the way teachers treat broader issues of relationships between the sexes in the classroom, and deal with questions and problems as they arise.

What is important is that the policy should specify what is to be communicated and identify where responsibility lies. There is parental right of withdrawal from sex lessons in both primary and secondary schools, though not, I repeat, from that which is part of national curriculum science.

Homosexuality in sex lessons

 Do you think it is right that pupils should be given information about homosexuality in their sex education lessons? Why is this a job for schools? I did see something about it when our governing body was asked to approve the syllabus, but I didn't take much notice till my daughter came home and described what she had been told. It is a very impressionable age – nearly 15 – and I feel there are some things they are better not knowing. Parents have said this to me also and think the sex lessons generally go too far. Anyway I thought the government had stopped a lot of that sort of thing. I now feel very confused. If you could spare the time could you enlighten me on our responsibilities and what the main issues in sex education are? I now realize I have been superficial and I don't feel able to deal with parents' questions.

 The basics of human reproduction are now for all age groups part of the national curriculum in science, and other aspects of sex education - emotional, social, moral, health - are the legal responsibility of governors. In a secondary school governors are *required* to ensure that this additional sex education is provided, approve the content and inform parents about it, and it must by law include information about HIV and AIDS. Teaching must be within a framework of morality and family life, easy to say but not so easy for teachers in today's world to manage sensitively. Parents have the right to withdraw their children, in practice also quite difficult to manage since a good school will reinforce the learning done in sex education lessons in other parts of the curriculum.

It sounds as if you do first need to become more familiar with the materials actually used in your school. Indeed, I am surprised that your governing body have not had a session at which staff discuss their proposals with you, and many secondary school governors also invite parents to come in and ask questions about what is being taught and see some of the materials. Interestingly, even parents who start by being shocked by the way things have changed since they were at school often come down on the side of information rather than innocence when they have talked it through.

Your comment about the government having stopped such instruction refers, I think, to the controversial Section 28 of the 1988 Local Government Act, which made it illegal for local authorities to 'promote homosexuality'. This does not, however, affect sex education given in schools. When you get beyond the strict wording of the law it is for the school to interpret its role, but it is scarcely possible to give young people enough information about HIV and AIDS to protect them without discussing homosexuality. Most teachers would say that in any case it is part of life, literature and history, and the inborn predisposition of a proportion of those whom pupils will meet, so cannot be ignored.

There is also an equal opportunities aspect. Homosexuals are not legally protected against discrimination in the same way as the law affords on race and gender issues. Nevertheless many equal opportunities policies adopted by employers and others condemn discrimination based on sexual orientation. Some schools will see this as another dimension of their role, namely, to promote tolerance and understanding of all groups in society, not only those who might face discrimination, but also at the other extreme those whose beliefs make it hard for them to accept homosexuality at all. A good school will want to encourage young people to discuss difficult issues and form opinions of their own.

You asked about other key issues. I believe the main one bothering teachers is how to interpret the morality and family life bit in the law. Some MPs and peers will have had a traditional view of what they were voting for. Others will have seen only an emphasis on loving and respecting relationships, condemning exploitation and accepting responsibility. Teachers say that a proportion of children come to school with experience you can't reconcile with traditional morality or even in some cases the more liberal kind. Schools must lead, not follow, and present good models, but how do you avoid giving children the impression that there is only one kind of good home, and causing them unease even about homes with single parents, grandparents or foster parents, never mind deeply controversial pairings? This is where governors can perhaps discuss with teachers how to find the best middle road, helping children to recognize essentials and see how all kinds of families build loving and responsible relationships.

Racist name-calling in the playground

Ours is a primary school with a variety of ethnic minorities represented and I often hear abusive racist remarks made in play when I am taking or collecting my child. They seem to go unchecked and almost to be accepted as though they had no meaning. I am only a very new parent governor and I don't know whether I should be within my rights to raise it but it does upset me, and my son says it is never corrected if it is just name-calling in the playground.

I should be very surprised if the head and staff did not take racism seriously and indeed if the school did not have an anti-racist policy. This, however, is not the same as 100% daily vigilance, and as you imply name-calling is especially serious if it has become so common as to be almost unconscious. It may, of course, not take place in the hearing of teachers. Even if children don't mean the words unkindly but just copy them parrot-fashion, it is amazing how cunning young children can be about identifying words which grown-ups don't like, and keeping a sanitized vocabulary for classroom or home. You should speak to your head about it, not in a spirit of criticism but one of enquiry as a new governor wanting to know how the school handles racism. Perhaps she will be able to show you some documents setting out what governors and/or staff have laid down, or perhaps your enquiry will reveal that it is time the issue was discussed again.

Considering a new reading scheme

There has been widespread dissatisfaction with the reading scheme in use at this first school (it was introduced by the previous head twenty-five years ago!) and radical changes are clearly in view. There is a suggestion that a committee should be set up to consider alternatives and decide on a policy. I have no objection as I know it is time-consuming and we must be grateful the head wants to bring governors in. My only worry is that an obvious choice will be a young lecturer from a local teacher training college who is very well-informed but she is also a bit modern for this rather traditional community and may even push for the abandonment of graded readers altogether.

Please don't be 'grateful' to be involved. It is essential that governors endorse a big curriculum change like changing reading policy, especially when it is so sensitively topical. As for the committee, it is a good idea to let an interested group of governors have a detailed look at alternatives, but it can't be a committee in the sense of one having delegated power, because curriculum decisions can't legally be delegated. Have a working party to do the spade work by all means, but the decision must be made – and not perfunctorily – by governors.

I doubt whether your college of education lecturer will have the overpowering influence you expect. Her expertise is valuable but I am sure there will be other governors representing your community who will restrain extreme views and be just as far out on the traditional side as she is on the modern. Just make sure the working party is balanced, and remember that in any case the full governing body makes the decision. Most schools nowadays have moved away from exclusive use of one reading method, and policies are much more likely to embrace a variety of techniques and materials.

Thought for the day – is it collective worship?

 Our staff – following a pre-OFSTED local inspection in which we were told we should 'cop it' for not having daily assemblies – are planning a 'thought for the day' programme. Every year group will take the same theme, quotation or anecdote and year heads will speak to it in their own way in a daily 15-minute slot before registration. It will of course have a moral element. Is this likely to meet the requirements of the law? In the different secondary school attended by my own child they have solved the problem by bringing in representatives of different denominations once a week to deliver a prayer and a hymn and short address, as it is a much smaller school and they are lucky enough to have a hall big enough, but gossip has it that the staff are very bolshie there and not prepared to take assemblies. Which of these – if either– is likely to be accepted?

 I doubt whether either would satisfy inspectors. Many secondary schools have acute problems – no big enough hall, ethnic mixes, and staff exercising their right to stand aside. The 'thought for the day' could end up with very little spiritual content and I am sure the law envisages a modestly participatory occasion with an element of faith and mystery. But at least your option is daily for everybody.

The denominations-in-turn will produce a Christian occasion, but one which is not daily for all pupils – and would be a burden on local clergy if it were – and which also could have very little participation. It is intended that it should be an *act* of worship. I know all the problems, but it would not help you to say that a practice will be accepted by OFSTED as fulfilling the law when the chances are small. Personally I would prefer an occasion which united the school in a recognizable ethos to farming the job out, even if it is on a less mystical wavelength, but I don't really think my opinion carries much weight.

Parents' rights in a church school

 This is a Roman Catholic school, but it attracts quite a number of non-Catholic pupils. As a parent governor I am often asked about such parents' position on worship and religious education. Can you please tell me their legal rights? There is also some moral pressure to attend Sunday services.

 There is no difference between county and voluntary-aided schools in the legal 'conscience clauses'. All parents in maintained schools have the right to withdraw their children from religious education or collective worship. They may if they wish arrange for religious education in accordance with their own faith to be given elsewhere, provided that it does not interfere unreasonably with attendance at school (the Act specifically refers to the beginning or end of a school session as suitable times).

In county schools a daily act of worship, broadly Christian in character, and religious education in accordance with a syllabus locally agreed in consultation with all faiths established in the area, are also compulsory. In church schools worship and RE will be in accordance with the beliefs of the denomination concerned, and assemblies may be held off school premises, e.g. in the church. The ethos of a church school is of course likely to be reflected in aspects of its work other than religious observance and teaching in the narrow sense, and parents who choose such a school should be realistic about this. But it is quite out of keeping with the spirit of the Act to put pressure on pupils to attend Sunday services. Section 9 provides that 'it shall not be required, as a condition of any pupil attending any maintained school, that he shall attend or abstain from attending any Sunday school or place of religious worship'. I appreciate that your school is not insisting on this as a condition of attendance, but the law is so clear in its principles that I should consider any kind of pressure undesirable.

Daily worship and a Muslim head

 As a head teacher I have several times been reminded of my duty to see that daily acts of Christian worship take place in this primary school. I am a Muslim. I understand that teachers cannot be required to involve themselves in religious observances to which they have conscientious objections. What is my position?

 The head teacher shares with the Secretary of State, the LEA and the governors overall responsibility for ensuring compliance with the main curriculum provisions of the 1988 Act, including those on religious education and worship. As far as collective worship is concerned it is the duty of the head, in consultation with the governors, to make the arrangements. The conscience clause which applies to teachers does not therefore apply to heads, but participation on a personal basis is not obligatory: the law does not say that the head has to *conduct* assemblies. A deputy or class teacher would be acceptable and in many schools the collective worship takes place in class or year groups. In any case it has been made clear that the law only requires a majority of assemblies to be Christian in character. Occasions for collective worship based on other faiths may be held at other times. In addition, if your school's ethnic character justifies it you may apply to your local Standing Advisory Committee on Religious Education for some modification of the legal requirement.

Withdrawing pupils from assembly in a Roman Catholic school

 This is a Roman Catholic school but many non-Catholic parents favour it because of its good academic reputation and discipline. A number of them withdraw their children from assembly. Is this correct? Surely if they choose us they are accepting our faith?

 I am afraid the legal right to withdraw children from RE and worship applies in county and voluntary schools alike.

Home-time class assemblies: are they legal?

 We don't have morning assembly, which I thought was now compulsory. It is a fairly small primary school so there is no problem of a hall big enough, but the head thinks it nice if each class has a quiet time at the end of the day with the teacher, talking about spiritual matters, having a prayer, and ending with a hymn. It is very good I think as it sends the children away in a calm and thoughtful frame of mind and prevents that 'just released' behaviour, but is it legal?

 Yes, what you describe totally satisfies the legal requirements, as long as the governors are happy about the arrangements proposed and formally approve them, since they are responsible for implementing the law on worship and RE. It is not now compulsory for the act of worship to be at the beginning of the day or to involve the whole school together, but it must take place every day. Parents must, of course, know what is happening so that if they wish to exercise their legal right of withdrawal they can do so. I am pleased – and I confess rather surprised – to hear that 'just released' behaviour is cured by this means!

Role of a special needs governor

 I am the special educational needs governor and I am naturally anxious to learn as much as I can about how the school deals with this responsibility so that I can contribute usefully at meetings and hopefully be helpful in time within the school. I already know quite a lot about the subject and I am very committed. My problem is that I have met with nothing but frustration in my efforts to spend time in school getting to grips with this subject. The staff regard me with suspicion and the head constantly makes excuses and puts me off. Surely when I have been designated for this role I have the right to go into the school to make a reality of it?

 It is indefensible that you should not have been made welcome in school on such a legitimate errand, or indeed that any governor's interest in visiting is not encouraged. The reason is undoubtedly fear and misunderstanding: fear on the part of the staff that you will interfere or criticize and fear in the head's mind that governors might get too knowledgeable and too intrusive. I am not excusing them but only observing that this sort of fear is common in the still evolving stage in the relationship of governors and teachers, and it helps to understand it. It also helps to remember that schools are under a lot of pressure and it is just at these times that everybody finds it hard to let others come near.

You ask about a 'right' to visit, but I'm afraid there is no right. Governors visit schools either by invitation or in fulfilment of a decision by the governing body that they should do so. In the latter case a governor can't be prevented from carrying out the wishes of governors as a whole and what you will have to do is to try and approach it this way. I think it would be different if the SEN governor idea were part of the law, but it is only a recommendation.

For a number of reasons I am not completely happy about the idea of one governor having individual responsibility for special needs, though I guess I am fighting heavy odds and shall soon have to accept that it is a lost cause. The governing body has a very specific responsibility for special needs, and there is a danger that they will relax and leave the designated colleague, once appointed, to battle on alone without much real status, as indeed you are doing. The whole governing body, in my view, after preliminary study by its curriculum working party if it has one, should discuss special needs regularly and have the appropriate staff report on a routine basis. Then if there is any problem needing attention or a visit by a governor or governors seems necessary they can put the weight of their corporate responsibility behind it. As I said this is what you must try to bring about.

If you have a good relationship with your chair, tell him/her about your difficulty and try to have included in the agenda the question of how the governing body is going to work, through you, to inform itself and involve itself in SEN. If the chair is unlikely to respond well, look for a few allies among other governors. It should not be approached as a personal problem involving your access to the school – that would be asking for a rebuff and for people to take up entrenched positions – but as a wholly routine matter of how the governing body is now going to use you in the context of its shared concern for SEN. Possibly the best first step would be to get appropriate staff to come to a governing body meeting to talk about their work: this is less threatening than what might now look like forced entry, and they might be reassured by the genuineness of governors' interest and the lack of any evidence that you wish to tell them how to do their job.

Understanding the curriculum: the importance of teachers

Like most governors I have little confidence discussing curriculum matters. I don't know the language or the issues, and sometimes don't see how we can contribute among people who have been in it all their working lives. Perhaps they feel the same! Part of the trouble is that we have little to do with teachers and they are certainly not easy with us when we do meet them. Any ideas?

You are absolutely right. Governors *must* build relationships with teachers. Heads could do a great deal more to brief teachers accurately on the role of governors, dispelling the myths and the fear and pointing to the positive gains from closer contact.

Ideally there should be a curriculum information item on every agenda, with a teacher to talk briefly to it, using them all in turn. It would be good practice for them and would help them to see governors in a different light as learners, apart from informing us. We should use every opportunity we get of co-opting teachers onto small groups, and we should all have a curriculum working party which is informing itself on the work of the school on a Forth Bridge basis. Even more than most governors' committees I would think this one should be open, with a core membership of course but with the date and the business communicated to all so that governors drop in when they have a free evening: ours is like that.

I am always urging that governing bodies have a system to involve all governors in regular school observation. Apart from better decisions and more effective ambassador duties, the benefit is in relationships built on shared enthusiasm, magic in all walks of life but especially with teachers since they don't often get it except from their own kind.

Social events with teachers should always be in your plan, but remember their workload and think about the occasional breakfast or tea to leave them their evening if you can. Occasions to talk about school issues without the pressure of an agenda are also excellent. Try to arrange for some governors to attend staff meetings on curriculum matters now and then, as observers and to learn of course.

Look after your teacher governors. They are your bridge to the staffroom. Ensure that their role on the governing body is a confident and fearless one: you may sometimes have to protect them against marginalization of their contribution. They *do* represent the staff and they *are* eligible to take part in all governors' duties where they don't stand to benefit from the outcome personally, and they may want help from other governors to establish this. Remember to ask them on appropriate occasions how the staff feel about something.

Finally, do remember to take an interest in teachers' welfare and working conditions and improve them when you can. Always make a point of congratulating as a governing body any teacher who has done something special, a curriculum initiative, out-of-school activity or extra qualification. Have a system under which all of you get to be on a teacher selection panel sometimes. I find I learn as much from that as anything apart from classroom observation.

I am glad to have a chance of saying some things which usually come up under other headings in the context of the curriculum. All we do as governors – managing money, looking after the building, making appointments, improving our teamwork and our meetings, building relationships – has meaning only in so far as it advances children's learning. Thank you, therefore, for this question.

4 Management

Local management of schools was introduced as a result of the Education Reform Act 1988. It did not just mean delegation of the school budget – though that for many was its most immediate impact – but all that went with it: appointments; staffing, that is, numbers, grades and pay; personnel functions including grievance, discipline and dismissal; and care and control of the premises.

The school budget is calculated in accordance with a local formula drawn up by the LEA within fairly strict guidelines from central government. A very high proportion of the money a school receives is based on the numbers of pupils in different age groups, so there is a strong emphasis for governors on recruitment and admission criteria. A much smaller proportion is calculated to take account of different circumstances and needs of schools. Governors set the budget, though they usually delegate its management to a committee. Generally their arrangements will allow discretion to the head or chair to authorize the movement of expenditure within specified limits from one budget heading to another. Governors may not plan for a deficit, but if one occurs it must be carried forward. Any surplus is also carried forward.

Staff salaries, books and equipment, miscellaneous supplies, water, light, heating and telephone, day-by-day repairs and maintenance, all come out of the school budget. Various LEA services, differing somewhat from one area to another, can be bought in by schools. Major capital works do not come out of the school budget but are carried out by the LEA in accordance with a prioritized major works programme. This programme is strictly limited by central government. Certain services are still provided centrally by the LEA.

Governors appoint heads and deputies. The director of education or his/her representative has a legal right to attend and advise, but governors alone choose. The choice of head teacher must be ratified by the full governing body.

Governors are also responsible for the selection of other staff. This function, however, they may delegate as they choose: to the head, the head and chair, the head and a nominee of the chair, or a governors' committee from whom members are drawn in turn to select with the head. Any of these options is legal as long as the governors formally choose it, but it is generally more satisfactory to spread the responsibility more widely so that all or most governors have experience. If the school has a system for governor involvement, such as governor of the month, attachment to a class or subject, this provides a ready-made rota.

Other management tasks of governors include establishing a pay policy and deciding on additional allowances for individual teachers; agreeing a policy on charges for school activities; and setting down behaviour guidelines. The latter do not cut across staff responsibility for responding day-by-day to breaches of discipline, but should form a framework of principles within which staff guidelines are drawn up. Governors increasingly also establish a separate policy on bullying.

Can we stop this poaching of children?

 I would appreciate your advice. I live just inside the border of an LEA with quite a few social problems and I am chair of governors at one of its 5 –11 schools. Our neighbouring LEA is a prosperous leafy suburb. I enclose a leaflet which a junior school over the border has been circulating house to house around our school. Two other local schools are also affected. As you will see it is a leaflet singing the praises of the out-borough school and inviting parents to consider it, strongly implying that a move at 7 from another school should not be ruled out. Our head has complained, without avail, though I believe one of the head teachers' associations condemns such practices. Are there any guidelines on how governors should respond? Ought we to be writing to the governors of the school concerned? Our teachers work so hard and this seems a blow below the belt.

 I understand your feelings and agree that this is not the pleasant behaviour of schools towards each other that we used to expect. We have the right to these feelings and a right to express them, and if your governing body (all of them – not just you. You can't speak for them) feel the same, there is no reason why you should not say so to the governors of the other school or even to an MP or two.

But I must add that there is absolutely nothing illegal in this action, indeed it is part of government policy to allow parents choice of school across LEA boundaries, and part of the logic of formula funding that schools should seek to increase their numbers. I actually heard an education minister challenged at a meeting on the policy of choice regardless of borders, and he asked what was wrong with allowing parents in a poor neighbourhood trying to get their children into a school in a 'better' one. But when competition amounts to deliberate poaching among families who may be already settled in a school it is hard to take.

I expect you often think about how best to promote the qualities you are proud of in your school, in an attempt to keep the loyalty of your own catchment area. In an answer to a governor concerned about competition from a GM school (Chapter 9, pages 206 and 207) with a very different ethos, I made some suggestions. I commend that answer to you. Here I will only say that we must believe in the sort of school we are, and not adopt an apologetic stance. A school which serves really well a community to which life has not given a great deal, respecting its families and having high expectations of its children, tackling their learning in partnership with parents, is a pearl beyond price, and need apologize for nothing. Extolling the benefits which localness can offer, both in terms of effective transitions and involvement of community, is the best way of selling such a school. Parents may wisely come to value influence above choice. It is only the school which is patronizing to families, however kindly, that need fear.

Must we take children from outside our area?

 We have considerable numbers of parents applying for their children to come to this church school from the county area bordering on our borough. We know it is only because they want their children to have a chance to go to a local secondary school with a high reputation and this would not be possible from the primary school nearest their homes. We think this is unfair because we cannot take all the local children who want to come. Are we within our rights to refuse? We are told we have to take them but this never used to be the case.

 Whatever criteria you have for admitting pupils to your school must be applied without discrimination to pupils from other LEA areas. This follows a clarification of the law in a court decision on a case in Greenwich a few years ago. As a church school you decide on admissions, but you must have published criteria which meet legal requirements. Criteria which excluded out-borough pupils as such would not be legal. If you give preference first to brothers and sisters, to churchgoers, and then to those living nearest, for instance, you must apply these principles regardless of LEA boundaries. I imagine your LEA allocates secondary places on a linked school basis, which is bound to cause some pressure on the primary schools which feed popular secondaries.

Organizing the appointment of a new head teacher

 It seems that regulations now require all governors to meet to appoint their selection panel for a head teacher, to decide what to do if the panel can't agree, and to approve the final choice if a recommendation is made. I don't think this is very practical: governors are busy people and it might be a long time before a quorum can be assured? Why not a staffing committee?

 The government, rightly in my view, have said these are decisions too important to delegate. There is also benefit in the *commitment* of the whole governing body to the choice afterwards, especially if problems ever arise to strain the relationship. It does not happen very often in a school, there is normally plenty of warning, and it is the most vital thing we do. The responsibility of the governors (not the chair) to choose (not passively accept) their representatives on the panel is emphasized, and that is good. Governors should think about the need for balance in the group and also try to involve all governors over the years. This is easy if they have already laid down a set of principles to guide them: arguing about Harry versus Jenny loses its sting if you have long ago decided to spread the responsibility among interest groups and ring the changes. As for the ratification meeting of all governors, fix this at the same time as you select the panel, and make it as soon after the likely interview date as possible.

Head teacher appointments – endorsement by the governing body

 I was interested when you referred to the whole governing body meeting to endorse the choice of head teacher. Surely all governors take great trouble over this process, with the panel at every stage being involved in decisions against criteria agreed beforehand. What is to be the nature of the panel's reporting procedure? What part can the whole governing body realistically play, when it has no knowledge of the process which led up to the decision? How can we ensure we don't lose good candidates while all this takes place? And how can we prevent the

procedures being abused by awkward governors who have their own
reasons for wanting to obstruct them? What will governors do if the
panel can't agree and what about the candidates meanwhile?

  I was simply reporting an amendment to the regulations which
required this. However, I would add that no process is proof
against behaviour by governors which is not sensible or against
individuals who use their position to obstruct it. I don't think a
governing body which has delegated the process of selection
so thoughtfully is then likely to use its power of ratification in
an arbitrary or wayward fashion. Nor is it likely to find it difficult
to exercise corporate pressure on a member stepping out of line:
governing bodies are used to this and in fact I get many
complaints that they are a bit too good at it!

The panel will briefly summarize their deliberations after the
final interviews, reminding the governors of the criteria and
saying something about the recommended candidate. The
governors will be able to question anything which seems to need
explanation. In the vast majority of cases I am sure they will be
happy with the process and endorse the choice, but I suggest
they will feel more ownership of it. In the rare case they may
make a valid point affecting the choice and perhaps even
occasionally prompt a reappraisal: one can't be too careful. If a
full meeting is planned at the time the panel is selected there
need be no long delay resulting in the loss of candidates, and
after all competing schools will be going through the same
process. As for what happens if the panel don't recommend an
appointment, this leads to unavoidable delay whoever has to
decide what to do next.

Do you want to know what the staff thought of the candidates?

  Usually short-listed candidates for a headship visit the school and
spend time with the senior staff before the final interviews. Do you
think it right for the panel to listen to any feedback from this occasion
to get staff impressions of the candidates?

  I do not think there is anything in the tablets of stone on this,
and I have been in arguments about it from time to time. I can
understand why people charged with this awesome task often

want feedback, because at some times in the process – and I have been involved three times – you want absolutely everything that can add to your store of wisdom and you gather crumbs like a starving bird. Psychometric testing, birthsigns, tealeaves! And you are desperate also for some idea of how your dear ones inside there who have to live with your decision feel.

But reason returns, and I will say straight out that I am against listening to any views from the tour of the school. It is an unscientific way of finding anything out, and therefore unfair. Not everybody will talk the same length of time to each candidate, and the context will be different for each. A single unconsidered remark could strike a chord or a chill. Nobody knows quite what the status of the event is. I don't know how you can defend the practice really, when you think how careful we all are about acting in the fairest possible way, giving everyone exactly the same time, planning the questions, being as attentive to the last as the first, constantly matching against the criteria. I think other governors and staff should feed in all they can when the job description and person specification are being written, and then leave those who have been elected to make the choice alone. Otherwise it makes nonsense of having a group to stay with it through every stage. Remember the fuss in a legal case where an appointment was overturned? One governor not previously involved was called in at the interview stage because one of the panel was ill and that was seen as an irregularity. Straining at a gnat and swallowing a camel?

Can the LEA pressurize us on the choice of head teacher?

 We are in the process of appointing a new head. We should have done so by now except that an LEA inspector threw a spanner in the works at the full governors' meeting held to endorse the choice of the selection panel. This inspector came to the interviews even though not invited and gave advice even though we didn't ask for it. (Can they do this?) We were unanimous that our deputy should be offered the post, but this inspector got really offensive about governors' habit of selecting deputies from the school for headships generally and being unenterprising and timid, and said we were closing our eyes to some much more interesting candidates. It is true there were good candidates but compared with our deputy they seemed to talk a lot of theory which

didn't convince us. There were other things we thought important,
such as that the inspector's favourites had not as it happened had
experience in a co-educational school or a tough inner city situation, as
ours is. The inspector repeated this to all the governors and some, being
in awe of 'authority', are reluctant to make a decision: we meet again
next week.

As you have a delegated budget the choice of head is yours
and yours alone. The law gives the Chief Education Officer or
his/her representative the right to be present and advise, but
you do not have to accept the advice, and this being so no LEA
person should lean too heavily. (In fact the right even to be
present was not in the original draft legislation and was
introduced during later stages.) It is true that there is some
evidence that governors are more likely to appoint internal
candidates, which may reflect fear of making a mistake in these
early days of responsibility. On the other hand, governors do in
many cases know the school and staff really well. We should all
listen carefully to expert advice – most of us need it – especially
on professional qualifications and experience, but please urge
your colleagues to make a decision one way or another now,
and assure them that they do not have to accept official advice
if they are confident in their panel's judgement.

Can we reject performance-related pay for teachers?

We have discussed the principle of pay allowances based on teaching
performance and don't like it. We are not satisfied that it has incentive
value and we believe that excellent teaching is not simply a product of
individual talent and application but of resourcing, ethos, good
management and teamwork. We also think such allowances are divisive.
What can we do?

You express very well a view held by many people in education
and as it happens I agree with you entirely. Attempts to
introduce merit pay before have encountered the same sort of
objections and in practice the allowances intended for this
purpose often found their way into payments for responsibility:
an excellent teacher will generally be given some special
responsibility. The simple answer to your question is that these

allowances are discretionary and you are not for the moment obliged to award any. Whether the government's belief in such allowances will lead to further pressure or compulsion remains to be seen. Whatever you decide to do should be part of an open and consistent pay policy.

Should we be consulted about switching a teacher?

 Is our head allowed to change a teacher from one class to another without reference to governors? A very popular year 6 teacher is to be given a younger junior class and the parents of pupils who would otherwise have gone to her in this important year are up in arms.

 Teachers are sometimes asked to teach another age group as part of their professional development and I should regard it in general as a day-by-day management decision within the head's role. If a head knows it is likely to be controversial, however, it might be wise to explain it to governors first: informed ambassadors are always helpful with parents.

Can a teacher be required to teach other subjects?

 Does a teacher have the right to refuse to teach subjects for which he/ she has no qualifications, specialist training or teaching experience? I have been asked to teach three subjects in addition to the one I specialize in, and they include RE. I am not a practising Christian.

 It depends on what it says in your contract. You will probably find there is some catch-all clause which obliges you to undertake any teaching duties requested by your head as the needs of your school dictate. If you are in any doubt when you have looked at this, consult your LEA or your union representative. I am not saying it is desirable that teachers should be asked to teach subjects other than those they are qualified in, but I am afraid quite a lot of it goes on. You cannot, however, be required to teach RE. This is a long-standing protection for teachers' freedom of conscience.

How the PTA spend their money

Could we have your views on this situation? We have a good PTA which has always raised a lot of money for the school. The governors often suggest something the school badly needs which they might like to donate. Recently we took over our own site maintenance and cleaning contract and governors are very anxious to work to higher standards in these areas and in particular to have the most modern equipment. We have a tight budget, and we asked the parents if they would consider making their next project a donation of equipment such as wet/dry vacuum cleaners, powered hedge clippers, litter collecting machines, etc. Our long-suffering parents have at last said enough's enough. They object to raising money for these basic and boring things which do not directly benefit the children, and a certain element also says they are not contributing to lost jobs locally for cleaners and ground staff.

That is it then is it not? If your parents feel like that they are quite entitled to say so. PTAs are everywhere buying textbooks, computers and even helping to pay for teachers, and many people feel sad about this, sad because it encourages underfunding of basics by those legally responsible and makes for inequalities between schools, and helpless because in the end parents will not see their children go without. But books and teachers don't seem so remote from children as hedgetrimmers, so that is where yours want to draw the line.

I must say I find it harder to see a logical line to draw now that schools have one budget whose distribution among so many needs is up to them. The budget is there for parents to see and if they once get into basic funding, what is the difference between keeping their children warm, buying set books or paying the water bill? Psychological only, but the psychology is important when you are dipping into your pocket and giving up your Saturdays. I don't think it is unnatural to want to choose something which is more directly for the children and in which you can take pleasure. As for the fear of machines doing people out of jobs, if you think it would help there is no reason why you should not state formally that you don't have any plans for reducing staff but want good equipment to make cleaning and grounds maintenance pleasanter jobs and to raise standards. But in the end it is up to the parents. Try to find something in your budget that is more appealing to them. It is all the same pocket.

Can parents fund a teacher?

 Next year's budget will result in the loss of 0.5 of a teacher, and this will mean there is no longer one teacher per age group. Parents are very unhappy about this, and they wish if possible to raise funds to pay for the extra half teacher. The governing body wishes to know whether this is legal. Some of us are not happy about accepting parental funding for necessities and also are concerned about parents who can't contribute.

 Many will share the reservations expressed about allowing parents to fund essentials. But you have asked whether it is legal and I know no legal objection. The school's budget, though it may notionally be based on certain expenditure heads' is, once delegated, a single sum for the governors to allocate as they wish. There is therefore no distinction in a fully delegated school between parents funding a teacher and contributing to the cost of library books or donating equipment.

There are practical issues, however. You must get sound advice on what the real cost of half a teacher is (i.e., taking into account NI contributions, pay during sickness plus supply cover and the like) and also any possible obligations in future on redundancy, etc., particularly if the consequence of parents paying for 0.5 means that you actually employ an established full-timer. It is a long-term commitment, and I think a discussion with your LEA would be helpful. They are still the employers in a county school, and although they cannot dictate how you spend your money they might well feel concern about parents taking on such a commitment and advise you accordingly. You will know I am sure that there can be no question of a 'levy' on parents. That *would* be illegal. No pressure at all must be put on parents to make contributions, and indeed it would be unwise to say anything which would make parents who can't afford it feel bad about it.

Why should we not give our head a car?

 We decided to give our head teacher a car. After all most people of that sort of seniority in business have company cars. (I am chair and a co-opted governor from business.) We had enough money for the purchase this year but next year and beyond our budget is likely to be down and we can't afford to increase the head's pay or, I think, (though we have yet to look at it in more detail) give any allowances to staff. This was therefore all we could do to show our appreciation of our head, though we recognized it was nothing like as good as a salary increase. I don't see that we have done anything wrong, but there is muttering among the staff who say it is unfair. What is your view?

 You have done nothing illegal or on certain conditions improper, but I think in the circumstances it was unwise. Governors should have an open pay policy (even if they have not currently any surplus) and it should take all staff into account. Any gift in kind should be part of that policy. I can understand the staff's concern, as I should not be happy about a gift to the head in circumstances where you have no policy on improvements for staff generally. I am not so sure either that you are right when you say it is nothing like as good as a pay increase. If you look at the annual payment necessary to borrow that sum privately for car purchase and replace the car periodically it is not a negligible sum. I do not know whether you have any commitment to replace the car when necessary or to treat any new head in the same way: if you have you may be in trouble with some future budgets unless you set something aside annually for the purpose.

It is too late to turn back now, but at least assure the staff that you will be working on a whole-school pay policy, that the basis of it will be fair and open, and that you will implement it as soon as conditions allow. Then go all out to find the necessary money from your budget.

No more redeployment?

 I am a teacher who has been made redundant because of falling rolls. The LEA has recommended me to other schools in the area and at one time this would have guaranteed redeployment. However I have been turned down by two governing bodies. Have they the right to do this? I know that in general they choose teachers but surely when it is a case of redeployment within the area they cannot stand on their rights?

 LEA redeployment schemes no longer apply to schools with delegated budgets. LEAs may recommend teachers who have become surplus to requirements in one school to the governing bodies of others, but the governors are under no obligation to accept them unless they have voluntarily entered into a redeployment agreement either with the LEA or with a group of schools in the area.

Charging for examination entries

 Parents have complained to us about being charged an examination fee for a pupil who truanted from all classes in the subject and did no course work, and of course failed. The head said we were entitled to charge.

 Under Section 108 of the 1988 Act governors may reclaim fees if the pupil without good reason has failed to meet the requirements of the exam. But I should have thought your school was somewhat negligent to let the matter get so far, if the facts are as stated. I should need more information to judge.

Can we ask parents for money when we have a surplus?

 As usual when we have our annual meeting we shall suggest ways in which parent-raised funds can be best used to help the school in the coming year. This is a bit difficult this year as we have a large carry-over in our budget. We expect to be criticized for asking parents for money when we seem so well placed.

It is hard to give a clear answer without knowing the reasons for your carry-over. I assume it is more than would normally be considered a prudent contingency fund. If you have deliberately set aside money for expenditure which has to be spread over several years there can be no reason for not explaining this to parents, surely, and they will appreciate that you are planning something of major benefit to the school. If on the other hand it is timidity or bad management, you have more of a problem, but even here honesty is the best policy: we are all new to money management on this scale. But you must not push parents too hard to fund items which you could easily afford. In these circumstances they will surely be much happier raising funds for some extra amenity for the children or something to further their own involvement in the school, e.g. furniture for a parents' room or corner. It is not a good idea to get into the habit of relying on parents for augmenting a school's normal expenditure though in most schools it is a sad necessity.

Can a governor become a bursar?

 Our chairman is shortly to retire early from the small firm where he is an accountant and the head, who gets on with him very well, has floated the idea that he might become a part-time bursar and look after the school accounts. Can you see any objection?

 If it is a paid job your colleague could not legally be chair, for a start. And any decision on the appointment would be yours as a governing body, not the head's alone. If your chair were happy to become and remain an ordinary governor in order to be able to accept the post, or if it were unpaid and seen as an honorary position, it would still in either case be for you to decide whether it was what you wanted, and you might look at the risk of undue influence, given his closeness to the head combined with the standing of a governor. It is in my view essential that decisions about money are made by the governing body or its duly elected finance committee and not by any one person: the expert's job is to make decisions easier for others to make, not to make them. With this caution it might work very well.

Budget transfers (virement)

Recently a major item of equipment in the technology department developed faults and was found to be not worth repairing. Clearly no provision had been made for such a large sum under the appropriate budget heading, and the head authorized replacement with a transfer of money from another heading where expenditure was running under estimates. Is this in order and should governors have been consulted?

The answer depends on what arrangements the governors have made to manage the budget. Money can certainly be moved from one category of spending to another (often called virement), the only question being who authorizes it. The governors may have delegated their responsibility to a finance committee, which would in turn have decided what happened if money needed to be spent outside a budget heading. Quite a common arrangement is to authorize the head to vire up to £X hundred or £X thousand without reference back, or to say that the chair of the finance committee could authorize virement. Whatever the arrangement, it should be absolutely clear. It seems that you are not concerned with the rightness of the decision in itself but with the proper way of doing things, and this is wise. In future you might use this experience to give the head a reasonable amount of discretion to meet unexpected expense and state clearly what is to be done on items above this limit.

Investing governors' funds

As the treasurer for the governing body of a small voluntary-aided school I hold the bulk of our funds in a premium interest account with the local bank. Can you tell me please: (a) is there any limitation on where I hold funds?; (b) can I within reason and normal business prudence chase the accounts with the highest interest?; and (c) is it possible for governing bodies to either reclaim tax paid on interest earned or to hold funds in a TESSA account?

I understand from our telephone conversation that the funds you hold are those raised by the governors from voluntary parent contributions and that they are used as necessary for minor building expenses within the governors' area of responsibility. You say that they are separate from the unofficial school fund, the LMS budget, and the larger sums held by the trustees which the diocese have set aside for a major project.

Within the general proviso that anyone responsible for other people's money is accountable for its prudent management, there are therefore no restrictions on where you invest it. You should ensure that your governors know what you are doing and endorse it.

As for tax, I am told that production of your instrument of government should be sufficient to exempt you from tax. A copy should be sent with any application to receive interest gross, and with any claim for refund of tax already paid which you address to the Inland Revenue. This exemption removes the advantage of investing in a TESSA account (though there is no reason why you should not) as there are plenty of comparable rates for non-taxpayers with no loss of benefit if you need to withdraw before the term of the investment expires.

If you were asking about a school's LMS budget I would have to reply that you would need to follow whatever guidelines your LEA issued (they do differ in detail) when they introduced the school chequebook scheme. These apply to voluntary as well as county schools.

Scrutiny of unofficial school funds accounts

You once wrote about the need for careful oversight of unofficial school funds and also the need for parents' organizations to keep proper accounts, audited and openly available. I am having great difficulty in persuading colleagues in our primary school that this really does apply to money raised by our parents who have no formal association but who fund-raise ad hoc and in effect under the headmistress's direction as and when necessary for a school purpose. Can you provide me with some further ammunition?

Yes, I am pleased to have a chance to return to this important matter. You can refer your head and fellow governors to the Audit Commission publication, *Adding Up the Sums*, which in paragraph 70 makes the clear statement 'All school voluntary funds should be administered to the same standard as public funds'. It goes on to say that they must of course be audited. It estimates that some £330 million of voluntarily raised money passed through schools in 1991–92, so we are talking about considerable sums. The booklet also estimates that about a quarter of schools handle voluntary funds in a way which would not pass muster if they were public money. There is also the point that *all* gifts to the school must be accounted for in the governors' annual report to parents.

The advice that voluntary funds must be monitored as rigorously as public funds is repeated in *Keeping Your Balance* (Audit Commission/OFSTED). This publication states 'Although such funds are not public money...parents and other benefactors are entitled to the same standards of stewardship for such funds'. One can expect the handling of voluntarily-raised funds to form part of any OFSTED inspection, so if only for this reason schools should look at their practice, and heads and staff should realize that it is for their own protection.

Can the head appoint all the teachers?

 I am a new governor so don't yet know what's what, but I did think we had some responsibility for appointing teachers. I find there is no governor involvement except that the head gets the chairman's endorsement after the event. Is this right?

 Governors are responsible for all staff appointments. They may delegate the role in any way they like for appointments below deputy, but this does not remove their responsibility. What happens in your school is legal *if* the governors have at some time decided that is what they want. I do not think it is desirable to delegate to that extent, partly because helping to select staff belongs with the curriculum responsibility, partly because it is good experience for governors. But you decide as a body.

Involvement in selecting staff

 Could you say what you consider to be the right system for involving governors in staff appointments? We always seem to have been casual about it: if the chair has not been available he has contacted a governor he knows and asked him or her to substitute. Sometimes no governor is present because the chair can't go and no-one else is available at short notice. When we appointed a deputy head it was suggested that the chair, vice-chair and a co-opted governor who happens to be a personnel officer should do it, but with no discussion, and no-one dissented. Now that we are approaching a new cycle perhaps we could be more correct.

 The function can be delegated, and there is not any 'correct' system: even when the arrangements are as unsatisfactory as those you describe, they are legal as long as the governing body as a whole has agreed to them. However if that agreement is passive, casual or vague, the spirit of the law is not being observed, since governors are *responsible* for appointments of teachers, and also solely responsible for head and deputy appointments once they are on LMS (sharing responsibility with the LEA in other cases). Therefore it is important that responsibility is consciously and thoughtfully assumed, with a system everyone accepts.

To take head and deputy appointments first. Normally these are not frequent and there is reasonable warning, so the governors can elect their team at the meeting before the event. It is best if it is a balanced team in terms of interest groups, for instance LEA member, parent, teacher or co-opted member. If the occasion arises again in the life of a governing body I think it is right to have a different team, with all governors being encouraged to take opportunities for training beforehand in good staff selection practice. My own LEA laid on an in-school training evening on interviewing for those on the panel to select our own new head, and some of the staff came for the experience.

I know some schools have appointments committees – legal, I repeat, if that is what they have agreed – but personally I do not favour it, whether for teaching or senior appointments: it is important that most governors have experience of interviewing and the feeling of commitment to the choice that goes with it.

As for teaching staff, governors may delegate choice to the head, or to the head with the chair if they wish, but it is not essential that it should be the chair and I personally feel that more governors should be involved. In this case governors need a system of some kind for sharing it out since there is usually less warning. Some have a committee as referred to above, comprising people who are interested and/or experienced and who are available. Others less formally have a list of such governors for the head or chair to call on. My own favoured system is to link the appointments rota to whatever structure the school has for involving governors regularly in the school – e.g. duty governor of the month system, special interest in a curriculum area (or perhaps a class in a primary school) – so that it is obvious who is the first choice. If that governor can't make the date he/she 'borrows' a session from a governor who *is* available and pays it back in that governor's month, class or subject.

Remember that teacher governors are eligible to take part provided they do not stand personally to gain from the outcome, for example apply for a vacancy caused. And it is a good idea to talk about arrangements for appointments before the need arises, at the first meeting of the academic year perhaps.

How is parents' money being spent?

   Parents in our school raise a lot of money which is just paid into school funds and used for whatever purposes the head and staff determine. Parents don't have any association and therefore no bank account. Sometimes a sum is transferred to buy day-by-day requirements like textbooks, but quite a lot just remains in the school fund to pay for hospitality, open day expenses, subsidies to help poorer pupils go on trips and miscellaneous needs that arise. There is no report to parents and they don't ask for one.

   Your remarkably quiescent parents may be happy, but you as governors are breaking the law in not giving full information about gifts to the school and how they were spent in your annual report to parents. Furthermore the Audit Commission has said that all unofficial school funds must be accounted for and audited as carefully as if they were taxpayers' money. Governors should see these accounts and they should be *informative*. It is not very satisfactory that the active parents don't have a bank account and is open to abuse. Any parent who buys a plant for 40p in the summer fair knows it is for the school and is entitled to know what such funds are spent on. Most parent organizations like to have some choice, anyway, in the use of their funds, even if they work, as many do, from a shopping list of the school's most urgent needs.

Head's role in the choice of a deputy

We are just about to appoint a new deputy and I foresee some disagreement. A senior teacher intends to apply and she and the head, both quite elderly, are very close. We expect to attract a strong field and most governors are anxious to get some new blood into a school which is well-respected but a bit dull. If the head, who has already made his feelings clear, is unwilling to accept our choice, should we give in?

I am sure you will not make up your mind until you have carefully weighed the merits of *all* the candidates against your criteria. Having said that, your dilemma is not uncommon. The head's advice must of course always be taken seriously, and head and deputy work so closely together that you need very strong reasons for setting that advice aside. I would say that the perceived need to bring in fresh perspectives *would* constitute a strong reason. It is not in the end the head's decision, and you must consider solely the interests of the school. Among those interests harmony is important, but most professionals will work with a well-chosen colleague even if they lost their favourite. By the way, on a related point, a retiring head should *never* influence the choice of a successor or canvass openly or otherwise for a candidate. I have had such a case brought to me, and it is unprofessional behaviour on the head's part, however tempting it may be.

Private building on the school site

Now that we are an LMS (county) school can we allow a private development on the site? We now have no hot school meals in our LEA, and a local couple who do party catering in people's homes are keen to supply the school. They would offer good terms, since the attraction for them is a base in a central situation (which we have) from which they could do other complementary work. They want to erect a light office and kitchen building and would pay rent.

The site of a county school belongs to the LEA. To use part of it for such a project would require a licence from them, and planning permission is also needed. I think you will find you also have to go through a competitive tendering procedure, even though the LEA has discontinued this particular service: they will advise you. I can see that the idea is attractive in that apart from the income you will get an amenity for the pupils. I am sure that you will consider all the implications for the school of having a business on site and also get good advice on the safeguards you should seek on responsibility for the building should the business fail, clear specifications and costs for the meals, and a mechanism for negotiating changes. The LEA staff will, I am sure, help you with this. You should also be sure that the chosen supplier has experience of this sort of catering – school meals are very different from dinner parties.

Unpaid leave for teachers

 Earlier this year we had a few requests for teachers to have permission to take a week's unpaid leave during term-time, and we granted them. Because of the kind of area we are in, many teachers' partners are in well-paid jobs and some go to frequent business conferences overseas. The number of requests now appears to be getting out of hand, yet we feel we can't say no to new requests which are no different from those we have agreed. Can we still establish a policy restricting such leave to exceptional circumstances? We shouldn't like permission to be taken for granted.

 You can establish guidelines for yourselves at any time, and I think you would be wise to do so, and publicize them. Your teachers' contracts will I am sure provide for compassionate leave to cover serious family illness and similar emergencies. Beyond this there may be a few cases where you feel you should use your discretion, but the fact that there may be a chance to go on a business trip with a partner or that a member of staff might like to take holidays when there are fewer crowds and more bargain offers does not seem to me to be a good enough reason to disrupt their classes.

Redundancy and incompetent teachers

Next year's budget looks like falling far short of our needs and the dread word redundancy is bound to come up. In my innocence as a fairly new parent governor I thought this would at least give us a chance to ease out one or two of our weaker staff – one in particular who is constantly complained of by parents. She does not do anything you could call unprofessional but her lessons are dreary and badly organized and she can't keep classes under control. When I mentioned this to the head teacher he nearly hit the roof and said I must never say anything like that again. I don't know a great deal about such matters, but I gathered from his response that you can't take the quality of the teacher into account. Does it make sense to get rid of good teachers when money must be saved, and leave incompetent ones untouched? Surely schools are there for children?

You are not the first and you will not be the last to ask that question. Most of us get frustrated sometimes because it is so hard to do anything about unsatisfactory teachers, a tiny minority but causing quite disproportionate damage. When cuts have to be made, however, it is vital, first, that everything should be done to avoid compulsory redundancy; second, that criteria should be established which are open and seen by all to be fair; and, third, that the needs of the curriculum are considered. An industrial tribunal ruled on one occasion that competence *could* be taken into account as a tie-breaker. In other words, when two people met the redundancy criteria with nothing else to choose between them, but even this limited pronouncement caused a lot of rumbles.

Remember that all employers under present employment law have to be pretty careful how they manage dismissals. Teachers have thus lost some of their *relative* advantages. I always reflect also when people grumble about the difficulty of getting rid of teachers how much more worrying it would be for us all if it were easy. Teachers are almost unique in their influence, and because they deal in ideas and values they are always potential victims of any kind of thought police. Without safeguards for their independence and security they – and the children in their care – could be extremely vulnerable.

It is a mistake to think anyway that nothing can be done about teacher quality. All teachers are regularly appraised and the appraisal used to further their professional development. There is support for newly qualified teachers and for any who are having difficulties. A great deal of counselling, support and in-service training is available, and in the last resort there are accepted procedures for establishing incompetence which could if the case is made lead to dismissal. Along the way, the procedures allow for positive outcomes arising from identification of problems, target-setting, etc., with the incentive that the matter is removed from the teacher's record if targetted improvements are made.

Who gets the LMS allowance when a pupil is excluded?

 If a pupil is permanently excluded from school, what happens to the allowance under LMS for his/her education?

 Before the Education Act 1993 the funding for the pupil remained with the original school for the rest of the financial year. The 1993 Act provided that funding should follow the child, and the appropriate proportion has to be paid by the excluding school to the school admitting the pupil. This. is covered by Section 262 of the Education Act 1993.

What can governors do about bullying?

 I am on the discipline committee of our governing body and I get very upset about the really nasty bullying incidents I hear of in the course of this work. It is not always just the cruelty that distresses me either but that so often the bullies seem to be really unhappy and inadequate kids with awful home lives. I have read books and other schools' materials, seen a video, talked to many people, but I am no nearer what we can do now, in our school.

 You give me a tough assignment as I have probably seen all the same materials as you and for the same reason. I assume that you as governors have established principles of behaviour policy on which staff codes are based, and that they leave nobody in doubt that in the hierarchy of offences this is near the top, not to be spoken of in the same tone of voice as breaches of dress code, bad language and cheek. That may sound naive, but sometimes an outsider can judge better how things sound to a child. In other words there must be no ground for any child to think that bullying is just one more thing teachers go on about.

Among all the things I have read and heard about bullying there are a few that have impressed me as central. The first is that you have to build an anti-bullying culture in which nobody is afraid to tell and nobody passes by on the other side, and in which every single child feels responsible for joining with others to confront bullies, condemning the action explicitly and getting an adult. This message can be supported not just in conduct codes and assemblies, but in RE, personal and social education, drama, English, history, wherever human behaviour is central.

Second, one must never cease to be vigilant about the curriculum and its relationship with behaviour. I know all schools try very hard to give successful experience to every child and to ensure that the curriculum is structured to that end.

The third point is that I personally think it helps a lot if there is just one named person to whom bullying can be reported, since that helps pupils distance the 'telling' from their normal peer relationships in subject and form groupings. It doesn't mean that they can't talk to a teacher they feel comfortable with, but only that they know they also have direct access, if they wish, to someone whose role it is to listen and who knows about bullies.

Fourth, you say what unhappy and inadequate people bullies often seem to be, and I don't think schools get anything like enough external support in counselling and helping disturbed young people. We should all carry on complaining about that. I know the 'no blame' approach has its strong advocates. I think bullying is an offence where it is sometimes possible, if difficult, to 'hate the sin and love the sinner', and indeed I try personally to apply that principle always with children. But I think also that this is very hard to get across to victims, with whom one's abhorrence of at least the sin should never be in any doubt. Finally, it cannot be emphasized too often that bringing bullying out into the open is a basic requirement of successful action. It thrives in concealment. Pupils should be encouraged to talk about it, to *define* it. It is so important that their definition should include the notion of exploiting superior strength – of any kind – or numbers, i.e. the power element; that it should encompass name-calling, teasing, exclusion, ostracism, making others feel different, extortion, as well as the usual physical violence. Defining bullying should extend to talking about telling, and how best to encourage it, and talking about how pupils in groups can face bullies, expose what they are doing in their presence and express disapproval. *Corporate* silence and fear create the conditions in which bullying can flourish.

Are tougher policies needed?

 Parents are beginning to press for tougher policies on disruptive pupils, and I must say that as our inspection draws near we wonder how the behaviour of our children will measure up. I do not think we have any more of these than formerly or more than other schools, but I suppose the emphasis on competition, testing, marketing, etc., and the pressure of formula funding spotlight them. Any advice?

 A common situation, partly for the reasons you give, partly because of the pressures on teachers and the increased social and economic stresses in families. I assume that you as governors have given proper priority to a considered behaviour policy, worked out with teachers, paying attention to positive strategies to promote good behaviour as well as sanctions. Keep this under review and always be on the look out for good models which you could learn from as a school.

Make sure that in your proper eagerness to emphasize the positive nature of discipline, however, you don't omit to tell parents that you do take certain kinds of anti-social behaviour seriously and deal firmly with them – some schools have gone so far down the road of expressing only positive expectations that they forget this explicit reassurance, and it makes current and prospective parents uneasy. Do you involve pupils enough in their own rule-making and rule-keeping? Is bullying the subject of clear policies, emphasizing openness and an anti-bullying culture in which all pupils share? Are your special needs provision and your pastoral care good? Finally, don't forget to remind parents (a) that support for the school's policies has to be provided by the home if they are to be successful; and (b) that outbreaks of disruptive behaviour, like learning problems, are no respecters of class but are likely to strike any home. It is not just a matter of 'Are slow learners/disruptive pupils holding your child back?'!

Make sure you give parents a chance to comment constructively on school policies at your annual meeting and other meetings with parents. It is too easy for parents to say the school should be tougher but they share an obligation with you to contribute to practical solutions to our *common* problems.

5 People in trouble

Governing bodies' much greater involvement in schools inevitably lands them with personal problems of various kinds. Some of these have a legal basis, a decision whether or not to suspend a teacher, for instance, or the determination of the future of an excluded pupil. Some do arise from the governors' legal personnel functions but stop far short of formality: the occasional head teacher involved in a minor indiscretion or a teacher under stress having a momentary lapse of judgement. Often it is the governors' duty to exercise some control over a member of their own team who is giving them all a bad name by some inappropriate behaviour in school, giving the head orders, upsetting the staff, gossiping about delicate matters. The poor chair often has the unenvied task of 'having a word' – but what if it is the chair who is the loose cannon?

When there is any possibility of a formal disciplinary action against a head or member of staff, however remote, governors must be extremely careful in what could be the early stages of a long saga. They must always remember that they could be having to determine an appeal – in which case there must be enough governors who are uncontaminated by knowledge or involvement to hear it. There is also the possibility of an aggrieved person going to an industrial tribunal, in which case the handling of the case will be under scrutiny and any procedural error could bring a decision in favour of the appellant even if the merits of the case are not in doubt. In particular events must be carefully logged by the committee charged with the task as soon as there is a possibility of disciplinary action; informal and formal warnings must be properly delivered, with appropriate target setting and follow up; and the principles of natural justice must be observed in allowing parties to see or hear what is being said about them and have the right of reply, accompanied by a friend if they wish.

Pupil exclusions require the same scrupulous procedures, since after the governors have confirmed a permanent exclusion the parents can appeal to an independent tribunal, and it would be bad for a school to be judged harsh or unjust by an outside body and not pleasant to have an excluded pupil reinstated by an outside body either. Governors should hear direct evidence as far as possible and not rely on second hand reports of what has been said already, and they must ensure that no governor directly involved – this could be a teacher governor, or a parent of the accused or a victim of the incidents – plays any part. The head must not be on the panel either in these cases.

Misbehaving governor colleagues are often very difficult to deal with, since a governing body has no sanctions. Often however the lapses occur from inexperience or role confusion, and the disapproval of the group will be keenly felt in these cases. Prevention is better than cure, and time spent sharing information about roles and good practice when visiting schools will always be well worth while.

Unwanted attentions

 As chair of a primary school governing body I need your help on what to do with two new parent governors whose enthusiasm is beyond question, but whose ill-judged interventions in school affairs are becoming an embarrassment or worse. They are gunning for a teacher who is having problems with class control, have been sitting in on her classes (which has only worsened her problems) and tried to get the governing body to rush in on this issue and bypass the procedures of support and enquiry within the school which are under way. They interfere in reading lessons because they have a bee in their bonnet about the reading scheme. This has been tried and tested and has been successfully used here for thirty years. They make suggestions bordering on instructions to teachers in the classroom on all sorts of things, from suggesting there is too much topic work to advocating more repressive discipline. Teachers are becoming anti-governor which is a pity.

 This is unacceptable behaviour and gives us all a bad name. It also sets back the partnership we must build with teachers. The parents concerned have good motives I am sure and may even be onto a few things that need changing, but there are a couple of basic things they must understand, in particular that individual governors have no power to inspect, make judgements or even give advice: these powers belong to the governing body as a whole.

Second, they must accept that individual governors do not have an automatic right to go into the school and visit lessons (though of course it is highly desirable that there should be arrangements for them to do so). Visits are either at the invitation of the head or in fulfilment of some decision made by the governing body, e.g. for a duty governor system or attachment to a class or subject, or that a group of governors should look into some issue in an organized way and report back.

Maybe if your governing body worked in these ways it would provide outlets for the interest and enthusiasm of individuals, as well as a framework of control. Ideally induction training for governors should include simple guidance by the LEA on relationships with the school and the corporate nature of governors' powers. Many LEA governor trainers now do team-training sessions with the whole governing body – could you request this for yours?

In the end, of course, the governing body itself is the best agency for establishing good habits. I might suggest that yours discusses the whole question of how it relates to the school, with a view to producing some guidelines, but I always hesitate to do this because in my experience such a suggestion is most eagerly taken up in schools where there is not much participation and where the main object of guidelines is to keep governors out! However, with the proper motives ground rules agreed by all are useful, and if it is done at the first meeting of a school year as part of a work plan, there is some chance that you can forestall bad habits.

Your letter does raise some questions in my mind about your school. Please forgive me if these are unfair questions. When there is a problem are you perhaps a bit too ready to be fobbed off with the statement that the school is dealing with it? Have you discussed your reading policy recently? Few people now want to go back to teaching reading solely by phonics, but there has been a trend towards combining different techniques, with phonics having a place. The date of your existing scheme and the suggestion of too much topic work makes me a little anxious about whether the school is in any kind of time-warp. Governors often 'meddle' because they are not involved at a more appropriate level and don't feel ownership of school policies, which must always be explained and justified to us. A governing body which has not grasped its role, or a head who has not accepted that role, will tempt individuals to go it alone. A governing body which is working well will know how to use and direct enthusiasm and concern.

New brooms raise the dust

 Our governing body has always worked well with the school. We now have two inexperienced parent governors, however, and they are causing havoc. They have an inflated view of their role, visit the school without notice, sit in on classes, and then bring up criticisms based on these visits at our meetings. They also raise parents' complaints at meetings without warning anybody. Next year we shall have some more new governors. They may well take their cue from these troublemakers. Our chairman is rather weak.

Not enough importance is attached to the induction of new governors, who may be well-meaning but still cause upsets. It is highly desirable that governors should spend some time seeing classes at work, but only through proper arrangements agreed by the governing body, always treating head and staff with courtesy. Governors should be responsible for their own ground rules and discuss at the first meeting of each year (or when welcoming new colleagues) how they will organize their work, also agreeing on basic principles of behaviour. The chair needs to play a part in welcoming and briefing newcomers. Yours sounds weak, and should only allow items to be raised without prior warning in emergency.

The first thing to emphasize is that individual governors have no power (teachers also need to know this) so come into the school to learn, not judge. Teachers should understand that it is in their interests that governors are familiar with classroom practice and so make informed contributions to decisions. The governing body should always consult head and staff about visiting arrangements.

But enthusiasm must be used, not smothered. New governors need help on how to get things raised if their enthusiasm is not to be killed stone dead. It is easy to explain why, if you intend to criticize a teacher, he/she must be allowed to attend with a friend, and why all procedures involving people's jobs must be beyond reproach to protect the school against an adverse decision in any form of appeal. But governors naturally feel aggrieved if they do not know the proper way to get things discussed, and advice on how *not* to do things must be followed up with constructive alternatives. If a concern is about one teacher, and is serious, the head could be told privately. A good example would be smacking, which is against the law and could get the teacher into trouble. Initially this is within the head's management role. But if the performance of a teacher contravenes a school policy (e.g. equal opportunities) ways must be found of bringing up that issue impersonally and involving that teacher along with others.

It is unfair to bring up parents' complaints at meetings without warning the head, but parent governors need help to deal with those concerns. A wise head will encourage this bridge-building activity and either facilitate a solution or, if the matter is of general concern, get it on the agenda. If a head continually stifles communication the governors as a whole may have to establish some guidelines to protect their individual members.

A problem of indiscretion

 This may seem a very trivial point but we have one co-opted governor who is well-known in our small community and who is indiscreet in what she says outside. I do not mean that she deliberately betrays confidential items discussed by the governors, but it is a very small and friendly school where governors are in and out a great deal, and of course we pick up quite a lot about the children and they themselves sometimes tell us quite private things about their homes. We also occasionally hear the odd exchange between staff which is better forgotten. Can we do anything to stop our colleague letting us down in this way? Should I ask the head to speak to her?

 If this were a parent helper in school I should suggest the head as the right person to tackle it, but it is mostly a mistake to put the head in a position to lecture governors. We should look after our own ground rules. Can you ask your chair to think about the best way to stop this bad habit? Your colleague means no harm I am sure but it does not reflect well on governors and could hurt people. Generally it is better if any guidance is given to the whole governing body as a routine matter: your chair could easily say that he/she has heard one or two things in the village which suggest that governors may have been abusing their free and easy relationship with the school, and remind them of the need to be professional. That is a good word, because it emphasizes the dignity and seriousness of a governor's role and the fact that they are part of a professional institution.

The induction of new governors deserves far more attention than we normally give it, and a good chair can do a great deal to stop some common troubles before they arise by reminding all governors, when the arrival of new colleagues makes it natural or at the beginning of the school year, of a few basic things. The need to apply the same professional standards as teachers to private things we may pick up in our visits to school or through our work as governors is an obvious one. Other points are that individually we have no power - only the governing body has power; that we go into school to learn and should behave courteously and avoid any interference in teachers' work; that we never bypass the head in any matter; and that we must be loyal to decisions we make together. Governor trainers might also remember these simple things in their induction courses.

Disciplining a misbehaving colleague

 How can a parent governor be disciplined? I was shocked when a parent governor colleague launched into an attack on the school for the way we had dealt with an incident involving her son.

 Why single out a parent governor? Governors from all interest groups behave inappropriately from time to time and in my experience the incidence is pretty evenly spread among them. However, to answer your question, and to start from the most extreme possibility, there is no chance of 'sacking' an elected governor even if it were desirable. Unless they become bankrupt or acquire a criminal conviction or fail to attend for six months without permission, they are with us for the full term of office or, in the case of a teacher, until they leave the school.

So we are left with training, guidance, and various forms of group pressure. Prevention is better than cure. Good induction courses should include guidance on the most common beginners' mistakes. Then there is the possibility of gentle guidance from the chair (preferably in the abstract, not waiting for a lapse) or better still sharing of ideas as a group on what constitute sensible ground rules to which all pledge themselves. The first meeting of the year is always a good time to discuss ways of working and behaving, and reminding ourselves of basic principles of co-operation. A skilled chair should be able to indicate some guidelines especially when new governors are present, on such things as avoiding personal issues, behaving well when visiting the school, not breaching confidentiality and being loyal to the school and to fellow governors outside meetings. If a bad single lapse does occur a friendly word of advice from the chair or a colleague in private may be the best way of preventing repeats. In the case of persistent offenders some more public rebuke may be necessary, and in extreme cases formal expressions of disapproval by the governing body are in order if a majority are of the same mind. Parent and teacher governors may also incur the disapproval of their constituency, and pressure from this source is often effective.

Good behaviour in the long term is a matter of the culture a governing body develops. This will not be an explicit set of rules, but is no less real for that. It will be communicated to new members almost without words. It will be sustained by example, implicit in the way people treat each other and underpinned by shared purposes. It will produce good induction practices and will be forgiving.

A parent governor's narrow view

As a head I find it tiresome that one of our parent governors looks at everything from the point of view of her own child and uses him as an example whatever we are discussing.

Many people worked hard in the 1960s and 1970s for parents to have a say in school affairs, and their direct experience is a valuable perspective. We should not under-rate it. If this governor is new this is the only way she can relate to the school as yet, but a broader view will come as she gets more involved. The governing body and the head can assist this process. It can be speeded up by giving her a chance to observe the school at work, especially if she is directed to aspects involving less fortunate children. A task which requires her to sound out parents on a particular issue will also raise her sights, and you can remember always to ask her at meetings what parents feel about this or that if you want to stress her representative role.

An over-zealous chair

I have just taken over the headship of this large voluntary-aided school. The chair is a strong personality who has become used to almost daily involvement in the school. He just walks in whenever he likes, goes into classes, looks at work, inspects registers and records, and I understand from staff has even been known to chip in during lessons and attempt to deal with badly behaved pupils. I think he means well, but the staff find it unnerving and I just think his view of his role is over the top. As for me, I try to be pleasant, but I object to his walking into my office without a by-your-leave, even at extremes when I am interviewing a parent with a problem or candidates for a post. I have put up a notice on my door saying 'Please do not enter the headmaster's room without an appointment'. The staff know it does not mean them, but unfortunately the vicar seems to think it does not apply to him either. My predecessor was timid, but I begin to understand why she took early retirement! Any advice?

I agree that the behaviour you describe is unacceptable. But you are dealing with someone who has a tremendous interest in the school and nothing but good intentions. Remember that. I do not like your notice very much because it is negative, because it *can't* in the nature of things be taken to apply to everybody (and a rule which can't be observed by all is not a good rule) and because no school, least of all a primary school, should give unwelcoming messages. You could say something at the entrance like: 'All visitors are welcome at St Mary's Primary School. Would you kindly call in the school office first? We shall do our best to arrange for the head teacher or member of staff to see you as soon as possible.' But I would have little hope that your regular guest would think it meant him.

You must think of ways of using goodwill rather than turning it away. In the short term try to find less troublesome ways of involving your chair - taking assemblies, being an extra pair of hands on a school outing, having planned sessions with you to talk about school issues. If you formally invite him for such a session he may get the message. After a friendly exchange in which you show respect for his experience where you can, you might be able to say 'Why don't we have a session like this every fortnight? It is so much better than my having to turn you away because I am interviewing or busy when you drop in.' Then fix a time.

You still have the problem of his going into classes, but in the longer term you must get the governors themselves to approach their work in a more organized way which will involve more of them in the school. This will provide a basis for ground rules on such matters as planning and focusing the visit, so that they go into a class with a purpose understood and accepted by the teacher, not disrupting the lesson and in no way undermining the teacher. The beginning of a school year is a good time to do this and if you have a governor who will understand what is involved as an ally, do use that person fully. If you are sufficiently devious you may even be able to give the chair the task of preparing some draft guidelines which he then discusses with you as well as other governors. That should give you the chance to say a few things you have wanted to say.

This may seem to you a roundabout way of getting there and without careful briefing the staff may see it as increasing the problem. They must understand that governors are here to stay, have (as a body, not individually) important responsibilities, and can be good ambassadors. In the end a chair goes 'over the top' only with the tacit consent of the rest and can only be dragged back by the rest. I get the impression that apart from him the governors are not very active, for instance in staff appointments: you should have a system for every governor to have this experience. At least then they all know what interviews are coming up, so perhaps you will be interrupted less often. Please don't allow the chair to dominate: impress on him that he is a teamleader and that the school needs the interest of all the governors.

An affair of the heart – and the head

Our head is having an affair with a class teacher. They are both married, but they are quite open about it in the school and at school events. Some governors are unhappy and a few parents have commented.

Staff members' private life is not your concern as long as it does not affect their professional work or decisions, and as long as they behave discreetly. It seems that in your case they are not behaving discreetly and I think it would be wise for your chair to have a private word. I hope this is all that is necessary.

Dealing with a parent's complaint: must it be such a big deal?

A parent sent a formal written complaint to the governors about a disciplinary decision affecting her child. We were quite prepared to set up an informal panel to consider the matter, but the head insisted that any investigation must be treated as a disciplinary action against him personally. Meanwhile the parent moved her child to another school so the matter was dropped, though we did take the opportunity to re-examine our behaviour policy. I have since wondered whether the head was right.

If every unwise judgement made or condoned by a professional in the course of his/her work were treated as a disciplinary matter, many people would spend a lot of time quite unnecessarily in formal hearings. It is absurd to suggest that there is nothing between formal personal discipline and accepting that everything that happens in a school is right. After all the head's judgement is on the line every time we determine a pupil exclusion case. It seems to me as if your head, through unwillingness to accept criticism of any kind, is putting pressure on you to drop the matter, knowing that you won't want it to escalate. I actually think you should have stuck to your guns and looked into the complaint even after the parents had withdrawn their children: it is a great pity that they felt they had to take such a step and gives a poor message to others. You were wise to use it as a chance to repair any gaps in your behaviour guidelines.

There is no formal *general* mechanism for parents to appeal against *school* decisions, though there are some specific appeal procedures, on curriculum and exclusion for instance. Nevertheless I believe that governors are able to look into any matter which has caused serious concern - obviously they must avoid interfering in trivialities - as part of their general responsibility for the conduct of the school and for relationships with parents. In a good partnership a head should be able to accept this as part of an ongoing dialogue about school policies which doesn't every time amount to a personal vote of no confidence.

A head loses her temper

Our head teacher recently lost her cool at a PTA meeting. She had been provoked by some parents' questions about school discipline policies which she found offensive. She also regarded them as interference in the management of the school. I can confirm that she was extremely rude, but we have discussed the matter as governors and, as she has admitted that she was ill-judged and apologized both to us and the PTA committee, we propose to take no action, though we recorded our concern and our hope that it would not recur. The school policies complained of, by the way, have our full support (though it is only fair to say that many parents don't agree). Unfortunately local councillors present who happen to be parents have talked to officers and urged that this was unprofessional conduct and should be the subject of disciplinary proceedings. The LEA are leaning on us to take the matter further. It is a county secondary school.

This is unfortunate as you obviously realize: failure to be self-controlled in a professional situation is not good news, but schools and their staffs are often under great strain these days. You have judged as governors that this isolated lapse should be regretted and forgotten, in an otherwise very effective head teacher. I consider that that is within your powers and that it should be the end of the matter. I guess you must have been worried to some extent by the publicity given to a case where LEA and governors were not agreed on the action to be taken on a head's alleged misdemeanour, but there were additional complications in that case which do not apply to yours, which is fairly simple and I would think not all that uncommon. At least the fuss will have made it even more unlikely that such an incident will be repeated. I would add that if a number of parents' disagree with (or don't understand?) important school discipline policies you should perhaps seek to re-open the matter or at least ensure that it has been thoroughly aired with parents. Defensiveness by heads over policies which parents find it hard to accept only stiffens opposition.

A teacher in trouble

 Sadly, a teacher at our school is to appear in court following a fight after a political argument in a local pub during the election campaign. Nobody was injured. We were not sure whether we should suspend the teacher immediately in advance of the hearing. A majority felt that we should not prejudge the outcome. I did not agree with this as it seemed to me that someone who, whatever the rights and wrongs, had been involved in violence, probably after drinking, was no fit person to teach children. What do you think?

 When a teacher is accused of an offence taking place off school premises and not in school time, immediate suspension is by no means automatic. The decision should be related to the seriousness of the alleged offence and to its relevance to the job of the person concerned. Obviously governors would be super-careful in any case involving abuse of children, for instance. It is not unknown where there are serious risks to children even for teachers to be dismissed before the case is heard, and in these circumstances, even if the teacher is found innocent, an industrial tribunal would not necessarily regard this as wrongful dismissal as long as they were satisfied that there had been such a risk, that the governors had acted in good faith, and that there had been reasonable evidence of guilt. I would agree with your colleagues that you should await the outcome.

How to deal with a teacher charged with a serious offence

 A teacher who was to have taken up a post with us this term has been charged with offences against boys. The incidents took place in the holidays, a hundred miles away, through a voluntary activity connected with cubs, nothing to do with our school or his previous school. He is suspended on full pay but we are being pressed to start enquiries leading to disciplinary proceedings. As governors we feel that we should not presume guilt and that we could be in trouble if we dismissed him and the charges were then proved unfounded. The case comes up quite soon anyway. We have a fully delegated budget.

 There are two issues here, first, whether governors should always await the outcome of legal proceedings before initiating disciplinary action (for fear of the outcome of wrongful dismissal appeals) and, second, the kind of misdemeanours in which governors should take the initiative at all.

On the first question there is abundant case-law to encourage employers to go ahead with disciplinary action where the misdemeanour occurs in the context of an employee's work and casts serious doubt on his suitability. Even if the teacher is acquitted in the courts, an industrial tribunal would not consider the dismissal wrongful solely because the courts had taken a different view. If the governors had proceeded in good faith and had acted reasonably throughout and, if, on the evidence available the dismissal itself was reasonable, governors need not be afraid. But the alleged offence took place far away and not in the context of the teacher's daily work and he is not yet established in your school.

The other question is more relevant in your case, however. Clearly the offence is of a type which has a strong bearing on this man's fitness to teach, and there should be no question of his taking up his post until the outcome of legal action is known: you are right to suspend him. At the same time I don't think it reasonable for governors to be expected to conduct an investigation into matters which occurred so far away and which did not involve the school in any way. The simplest answer is to maintain suspension until the case has been heard. This is my opinion. However there may be circumstances I don't know, and you would be wise to work closely with your LEA (though in the last resort it is your decision). In any matter which carries financial risks, the school carries the can if it has acted against LEA advice, but if the LEA has supported governors in, e.g., a dismissal, they pay any costs arising from a successful appeal.

Corporal punishment: why was I muzzled?

I was very upset to hear from my son that a teacher had administered a severe slippering to a classmate. Other pupils confirmed the story. I brought it up at the next governors' meeting two weeks later under 'Any other business' and was ruled out-of-order. I now hear that the teacher had already been severely reprimanded. But surely I should not have been muzzled.

It *is* an urgent and a serious matter, and you should have ensured without waiting for a meeting that your head teacher was privately informed at once and asked to investigate. Evidently he/she got to know anyway. You should never bring up a new item at a meeting without warning the head as well as getting the chair's permission, and if it involves publicly accusing a teacher of a misdemeanour you must ensure that the teacher is present to hear what is said and given a chance to reply and bring a friend. You also have to be careful in any matter which may result in a disciplinary action that your facts are correct and that fair procedures are scrupulously observed, as the consequences of procedural error could be serious. In a case of this kind, for the reasons given and because of the urgency, it is normally better for the facts to be established by internal enquiry first. A teacher who administers corporal punishment needs to be warned at once that such action exposes him/her to being sued for assault.

Can we overlook an isolated smack?

 One of our teachers has struck a nine-year-old child across the head. It was not a heavy blow and the parents have not complained. The provocation was extreme and the teacher concerned had just returned to work after a serious illness. We all think he is showing signs of strain. In this inner city school life is not easy anyway. It is the first incident of its kind and the teacher is clearly sorry.

What do we have to do? I am afraid the governors are unlikely to be united. We have the usual mixture: people who do not see anything wrong with smacking, at least two who want to make a big deal of it, and the rest who could probably live with the idea that it was unfortunate but that as a one-off incident we could overlook it.

 I assume you have full delegation, in which case it is the governors' responsibility to decide what to do. I don't think you have the option of 'overlooking' the incident, if only because as the law stands you put the teacher at risk by not at least spelling out the possible consequences. This is because the 'banning' of corporal punishment in the 1986 Act took the form of removing teachers' protection against legal action for assault, i.e. it would not be a defence that the action was taken in the course of a teacher's duty to maintain good behaviour. If these parents chose to sue, you could not do much to help your teacher, so you must ensure that he understands the consequences of doing the same thing again and is in no doubt that you take it seriously. As to how seriously, I cannot decide that for you. My own judgement – and I speak as someone who finds physical punishment at school abhorrent – is that disciplinary procedures would be excessive for this single offence, but that the governors should communicate their concern fairly formally to the teacher, explain the risks he runs, and warn that further incidents would be treated more seriously.

Who suspends a teacher?

 Our chair approved the head's decision to suspend a teacher – on full pay, pending the outcome of a court case. Surely we should all have been involved?

If the *governors* are contemplating suspending a teacher it should be a decision made by a disciplinary panel elected by the whole governing body. But either the head or the governors may suspend a teacher, and if the head initiates the suspension it is not strictly necessary for him to consult the governors in advance at all. Many heads would talk to the chair on an informal basis for their own reassurance: being a sounding board or a hand to hold through a difficult action is one of the chair's commonest roles, but it cannot be regarded as a formal endorsement by governors. I think it might still, however, make it unwise for the chair to be subsequently involved in any appeal against the suspension or against further action, if any. Remember that suspension is normally regarded as a neutral act and does not in any way prejudge later decisions. Suspension on full pay is often carried out when a teacher is accused of some behaviour which would be a danger to pupils, even when guilt has not been established. In these cases there is not usually much time to waste.

Two's company

 We have two teachers, a man and a woman, who have a very close relationship. Indeed I believe they have been living together for some time. That is no concern of ours and they are good teachers. The trouble is that they teach between them the two top classes of juniors (it is a junior mixed and infants school) which occupy two of three classrooms in a self-contained block. It was once a separate infants school. While they work very well together and bring together the two year groups in an imaginative way, they don't work well with anyone else. The teachers in charge of the third class have never stayed long – they have either successfully appealed for another class or left us, and some have told individual governors that it is because the two I mentioned make them feel excluded. Even students on teaching practice have been unhappy with these teachers. What can we do?

 Teachers' private lives are certainly no concern of governors when their professional competence is not in question. In this case, however, a personal relationship *is* significant professionally, since it makes your two teachers ineffective members of a team. It is not acceptable that one class in the school has had to endure so many changes, and if the charge of non-co-operation with other staff and students arises from solid evidence, it is a failure of management to have endured it so long.

It is easy to think of ways of tinkering with accommodation and organization which diminish the problem: regular changes of class for all junior staff, planned joint activities involving other pairs of classes as well, some team teaching and different use of class spaces. (There must be four classrooms in the other building, so I assume there is some non-obvious reason for using it in the somewhat unusual way you do.)

But I would never advocate using space and systems to avoid tackling human problems, though it is done too often. (I was once shown a school being pulled down and told it was the only way they could get rid of the head!) This is clearly a management responsibility and governors' role is, as so often, to warn. The head must make it clear to both teachers that, while their abilities both individually and as a duo are appreciated, their failure to work with others is not. If and when their willingness to co-operate is established it can then be underpinned with organizational support, especially links with other classes.

If this problem ever escalates and comes before governors you must be careful to observe all the correct procedures (your LEA will have guidelines) applying to discipline of staff, to protect yourselves, should it go so far, in a grievance action or an appeal against dismissal. I once heard of a case just like this which escalated into a very big issue, with unions heavily involved, etc. simply because a head had been too nice to tackle it before it went too far.

A teacher faces investigation

 Our personnel committee is about to start investigations which will probably lead to disciplinary action against a teacher. It is an allegation of sexual misconduct with a fifteen-year-old girl, but the evidence is not conclusive. A number of things worry me about the way our head is advising us. First, he wants the governing body to suspend the teacher on full-pay first, which seems to me assuming guilt. Second, he wants a full statement of the problems with this teacher to be circulated to all governors. Third, he has said our teacher governor should not be on the subcommittee when it is considering the matter and must be replaced.

Suspension on full pay is held to be a neutral act, i.e. not presuming anything, though recently with the growing number of alleged abuse cases teachers have become more reluctant to accept it as neutral. Nevertheless there will be some circumstances when the nature of the alleged misdemeanour makes it wise. The head can suspend a teacher without reference to governors, but since this case is going to require investigation with a view to disciplinary action, your head is wise to involve the personnel committee in the decision. No initial investigation in a disciplinary case should ever be undertaken by all the governors, because if there is an appeal enough governors should be innocent of previous involvement to hear it. For similar reasons it would be wrong to circulate all governors with any kind of 'agenda' for the disciplinary action if this could be held to influence them. Your committee should make the decision on suspension and handle all information about the case. There is no reason why a teacher governor should not be on a committee dealing with teacher discipline if the governors as a whole wish it, the teacher concerned has no direct personal involvement in the issue ('more than the generality of teachers') and the teacher feels comfortable personally about taking part.

Persuading parents to move pupils who have seriously misbehaved

 This is a large – and pretty tough – comprehensive school and I am a new parent governor. We have quite a lot of bad behaviour and some exclusions. One thing I have been arguing with a fellow governor about is a practice the head and deputies have of trying to persuade parents, when somebody has 'got to the end of the road' here, to ask for the child to be moved to another school straight away, where the alternative would be expulsion. It is explained to them that the school will not send the pupil off with a bad report and that there is a better chance of getting a place somewhere else and a fresh start than if the child had actually been expelled. This seems to me quite sensible and in the child's interest, but my colleague thinks it is a fudge. Who is right?

 I can understand your feelings as a parent, but I am afraid I agree with your colleague. Although the head and staff may mean well, they are in effect getting rid of a pupil without any of the safeguards which would apply if that pupil were excluded. The parents are told there is no other option, but in fact they would have rights of an in-school hearing and an independent appeal. You have to ask yourself how you would feel if it then emerged that a child had been falsely accused, and had no chance to prove it.

This practice has attracted quite a bit of criticism.

Reinstatement of excluded pupils: who decides?

To 'streamline' consideration of exclusion cases the head has suggested that governors should delegate the task of deciding whether or not to re-instate an excluded pupil to the chairman. He stresses the need for a speedy decision in these cases which of course we agree with, points out that he always works closely with the chairman and will give him all the information to make a judgement. I think it is dangerous to let one person decide.

It *is* dangerous, and in the vital decision on the fate of an excluded pupil it is also illegal. Regulation 26(4) of Statutory Instrument 1503 1989 says that this task may not be delegated to an individual, but only to a committee consisting of not less than three governors, and that the head may not be a member. This establishes clearly the principle that the head should stand aside from the decision, and it is important that those who make the decision have access to as much direct evidence as possible about the events leading up to the exclusion. It is also vital that none of those who determine the case have previous involvement in decisions about the pupil or in the events leading up to the exclusion. Governors would therefore be wise to have some reserves elected by name, as exclusion decisions can't wait for a full meeting, and it is essential that governors elect the group. A governor too involved in the case should not be on an exclusion panel.

A harsh decision and a fellow parent's feelings

 I am a parent governor of a comprehensive. I have just been approached by a parent whose child has had a permanent exclusion letter. At first I said I did not think it was proper for me to talk to her, but she was almost hysterical and as a parent myself I could not turn her away. I realize I have probably disqualified myself from any further involvement. Now I am glad I listened but even more distressed. I agree, and so does the mother, that the girl behaved very badly towards one teacher whom she cannot stand, and the girl has a fiery temper, but she has an unblemished record so far and is brilliant at her work, taking GCSEs this year. The things that upset me were first of all that she was told that governors always supported the staff so appealing was a waste of time, and second, that the girl's record was neither here nor there. The deputy head said all this. I feel very upset that a fellow parent has been spoken to like this and also that we as governors have been so misrepresented. What can I do?

 I think you have put yourself outside the formal hearing procedure, but I am sure the other parent governors will do their stuff. You can urge the parent to take advantage of her right to be heard and also encourage her to go to the next stage of independent appeal if necessary. You can assure her – assuming you can put your hand on your heart and say so – that the governors do not support the staff blindly and that she will get a fair hearing, with the governors entitled to require reinstatement if they think the treatment too harsh. The law clearly indicates that missing public examinations should be taken very seriously: if the worst happens and exams are near, schools often set and mark work for the time remaining and allow the pupil to take the exams at school. Otherwise the LEA may make some arrangements for her to take them elsewhere.

The deputy head's statement, whatever the provocation (and you must allow for the fact that you may not have the whole story, as I am sure you know), was not acceptable. I doubt whether he was reflecting school policy, and unfortunately staff do not always have the chance to familiarize themselves with the law and the role of governors. I think at the very least that you must express your concern to the head that such a statement was made on behalf of the school, and point out how badly it reflects on governors. You might also just check that whatever information goes to parents about disciplinary procedures – in your prospectus, handbook or annual report to parents, for instance – says very plainly that they have a right to make representations to governors against permanent exclusion as well as a formal appeal, and will be given a fair hearing.

A difficult exclusion case

 A boy was excluded from this junior school for two weeks for bullying. There had been some particularly nasty incidents and one of the parent governors on our discipline committee was given information by victims' parents and also approached several times by the boy's somewhat aggressive father who was trying to say it was all fabricated. After discussion between the head and the governors on the committee it was agreed to re-admit the boy on daily report on the understanding that he would not be given a second chance. After a week there was another absolutely vicious attack on a much younger boy at home-time and the same day (before this came to light) a break-in after school when this boy was caught treating school pets with indescribable cruelty. He has been permanently excluded and his parents have asked for a hearing. Can the parent governor I referred to take part in this and in the decision about the boy's case?

 This in-school hearing must be conducted on the same principles as an appeal, and the first of these is that no-one involved in the earlier decision (and it sounds as if all members of your relevant committee may have been so involved) or the incidents leading up to the decision may serve. Governors would be well advised (because legally they *must* elect their committees) to elect a second group of governors, without waiting for the need to arise, and also a couple of reserves (in case someone cannot attend at short notice) to shadow the standing committee and take over in a two-stage exclusion such as you describe. The child clearly needs skilled help. I hope whatever happens you will be able to secure this. I hope too that as governors you have a clear policy on bullying and as far as possible try to involve all pupils in an anti-bullying campaign.

6 Representation and communication

In a broad sense the whole governing body represents the public and should aim to improve in every way the school community's understanding of the aims, methods and achievements of the school. It is also the whole governing body's task to report to parents annually on its work and to arrange a meeting for them to discuss the report and the running of the school.

This chapter is concerned also, however, with the representative roles of the different interests on the governing body. Experience suggests that parent and teacher governors in particular are often confused about their relationship with those who elected them. They believe they do have a representative role but don't know how far it extends and how to reconcile it with loyalty to colleagues in the occasional case where the expressed views of their interest group are in conflict with the interests of the school as they see them. Often they are told that they are no more responsible for communicating with their 'constituents' than other governors, that it is not their job to seek the views of those constituents or report back to them. Occasionally, too, they are excluded from certain tasks on the ground that they are too close to parent or teacher interests for this or that involvement to be proper. It is often the same people who display both these attitudes, which is extraordinary as they contradict each other. Part of the problem is that established interests on the governing body may subconsciously fear the power of representative people. Yet other governors representing the LEA, the church, the community also sometimes ask what their distinctive angle and role should be.

The first thing to say is that the *primary* loyalty of every governor must be to the governing body as a whole and thus to the welfare of the school as they, in open debate with colleagues at properly conducted meetings and with the benefit of all available information, see it. I mention 'debate', 'properly conducted meetings' and 'information' because, while different interest groups are deliberately brought together in a governing body to ensure its breadth and variety, the end product also reflects their influence on each other and their shared knowledge.

This means that no governor can ever be a *delegate*, that is someone who comes to a group with a predetermined line and instructions on how to vote. In the end if there is a conflict between what the constituents say and the governor's own view about the interest of the whole school, the latter must prevail.

That is not to say, however, that governors do not have a representative role, a second loyalty to the group they represent and a duty to listen to them, convey their concerns and keep them informed. It is this process which is often challenged and sometimes obstructed. The act of election makes the representative role especially strong for teachers and parents, but appointed and co-opted governors also have a duty to communicate with and on behalf of the LEA, the church or the wider community, not necessarily agreeing with their views but prepared to listen to them and ready to pass them on. Many LEAs for instance have now given up any attempt to confine appointments to party adherents, but I would still consider that an LEA governor should be familiar with the policies of the LEA (as distinct from the ruling party).

The representative role consists entirely in communication, and the head and the rest of the governors should make it as easy as possible for individuals to communicate. That means not overdoing the confidential classification (which should only be used to protect individual privacy), facilitating parent contact with parents as a whole, making space for representative governors to convey any concerns of their group in debate, not being over-sensitive to the expression of views which the head or other governors may not in some cases welcome, and accepting that parent governors may have to act as a bridge for individual parents with anxieties they feel unable to bring to the school without a hand to hold. The head has a major role to play in encouraging teacher governors to bring staffroom concerns to governors and also contribute fearlessly to debate at meetings. The head in the end has far more to gain from the healthy input of teachers than to lose from any minor embarrassments along the way.

As for participation in 'sensitive' decisions (also dealt with in Chapter 8) it needs only to be said here that every governor has an equal right to participate in everything, save only for the rules about direct personal interest in (i.e. opportunity to gain from) the outcome.

Role of a co-opted governor

My local comprehensive has vacancies for co-opted governors in the autumn. My own children attended the school in their time, and I have continued to take an interest in it, gone to open days and special events, and kept up my covenant to help its funds. I have now taken voluntary redundancy from a local electronics firm and at little over fifty I am still active and very much involved in the life of the town. I am keen on sport and amateur dramatics, on the residents' committee, and I work voluntarily at the local hospital. I am not sure what qualities are called for in a school governor or whether I would have the necessary expertise. Also sometimes co-opted governors are referred to here as community governors and I am not sure what this means in terms of accountability, contacts, etc. Could you please advise me on my role?

In a sense all governors represent the local community, since as a body they are there to represent the public in school decision making. Their legal position arises from the fact that schools are financed from public funds and from the belief that their quality affects society as a whole. School governors are not required to have any educational expertise, though it is essential that they are interested in education and prepared to take advantage both of training opportunities and of involvement in the school to improve their understanding of their role.

A co-opted governor (who is chosen by the other governors) does in a special sense represent the local community in as much as other governors are elected by the parents or the staff, or appointed by the LEA or the foundation in the case of a voluntary school. A person chosen for a broader perspective would naturally bring the interest of the neighbourhood to bear on school matters, though there is no formal requirement to consult. You would, however, participate in exactly the same way as other governors in all the corporate duties of the governing body: helping to form curriculum policy, taking responsibility for the budget, selecting staff, and sometimes determining disputes. Then as an individual it would be your special concern to watch the impact made on the neighbourhood by the school, warning of possible problems; helping to promote co-operation with local groups and avoid conflict; securing a better understanding of the school among its neighbours; and looking out for ways in which the community could contribute to the curriculum and activities of the school and also how the school could open its facilities to other users.

With some spare time, your continuing interest in the school, your professional experience and your broad sporting, social and cultural interests, I am sure you would be an excellent governor and able to help the school in many practical ways.

A better annual report

 I know you think the main factor in a well-attended annual meeting is the quality of the report. What are the main features of a good report?

 It should be written by the governors and reflect *their* perspective and concerns, giving parents some idea of how governors organize their work and make their decisions. It should be different from other reports the school produces and highlight matters of concern to parents - the safety and happiness of their children, health and sex education, behaviour policy, personal and social education, out-of-school activities.

Ideally the report should be a team effort with contributions from individual governors and information about them. It should be written in simple language with a friendly tone, illuminating for parents what children learn in school. It should be easy on the eye, with well-spaced text and some illustrations. Children's work is always popular, but it should be in proportion and relevant. Otherwise the report could easily look like a school magazine. Parents should be encouraged to take an interest in the work of governors.

Above all the report should look forward as well as backward and invite parents' ideas and concern about problems the school will have to face in the future. There is no participation in the past, and however much parents may welcome the information they are given about things that have already happened, they will not feel the need to come and discuss them as well. They will come if they feel needed.

What sort of concerns can be raised at annual parents' meetings?

 At our annual parents' meeting quite a large group of parents expressed strong disapproval of the practice of keeping pupils in long detentions during the winter months when many of them would have to walk home in darkness along lonely roads where we have already had some nasty incidents. The head refused to respond to the criticism on two grounds: first, that the meeting was not quorate; and, second, that it was a day-by-day management issue and as such not appropriate to a meeting with governors or within parents' right to challenge. Was he correct?

 Incorrect on all counts I am afraid. First, there is a lot of misunderstanding about the 'quorum' issue. It is not correct to refer to a meeting of this kind as 'inquorate'. There is no rule on a quorum for the annual meeting. All the law says is that if parents equivalent to at least 20% of the school roll attend they can pass formal resolutions on which they are legally entitled to a response. It does not say they cannot express opinions or that the school should not respond if attendance is lower. The fact that it is not *obliged* to does not alter the folly of stone-walling on any important matter, whatever the attendance. What a way to encourage better attendances anyway!

Second, the annual meeting can raise any matter concerning the running of the school: this is explicit in the Act.

Third, although response to misbehaviour day-by-day is an internal matter for the head and staff, governors do have a right to lay down general guidelines on discipline, which could well include something about the safety of pupils being over-riding. They also have general responsibility to represent the community and if any action by the school causes widespread concern they should ensure that it is considered and receives a proper response. Governors must always of course recognize how difficult some of these issues are for schools and accept that nearly all sanctions could raise objections on one ground or another. Some schools write informing parents about detentions and at the same time reminding them that it is their responsibility to get their sons and daughters safely home, but I always feel that this latter is not a realistic option for large numbers these days.

Annual parents meeting: must it be in the summer?

 Are we obliged to have our annual meeting for parents in the summer term? It always seems to be harder to get people to meetings on fine evenings and this term is in any case full of other pressures on schools – tests, reports, exams, summer fetes, sports, treats for those leaving, etc.

 Governors can have this meeting at any time as long as they don't fail to have one in any school year. In practice this means that you can't move from summer to autumn in one step, which is probably one reason why so many have stuck with a summer date. The 1986 Act which introduced this meeting said that the first had to take place before the end of the academic year in which the Act took effect, which meant summer term. The end of the school year does seem natural and from the point of view of reviewing the expenditure and seeing how the budget affects school policies in September it is good. But there are some arguments against, apart from the one you have given. Exam results in secondary schools are a year old, new parents have to wait a long time for a meeting, and parents of leavers may have lost interest. If you do decide to change you will have to have shorter intervals for at least two years and inevitably this means that on some annual themes there will not be any fresh news. But it is worth it if it results in meeting at a time of year which suits your school better.

Must we publish home addresses?

 A parent has queried our refusal to give home addresses and telephone numbers for governors, or at least for the chair. We feel that it is an intrusion on their privacy. What is the general practice and is there any regulation about it? We always forward any correspondence sent care of the school.

 Governors are required to publish the address of the chair and clerk in their annual report to parents. This is stated in the 1986 Education Act. I feel satisfied this is intended to mean home address: otherwise why say it? As for other governors, practice varies. Many schools do give home addresses for all, and I myself think this gives a good impression, even if it is not compulsory. I think that if you take on a public office you should be willing to be accessible. I do realize that one risks being bothered constantly about trivialities, but which is worse, being bothered too much or being unavailable when something really serious needs attention outside school hours or terms? Even in school time there may be cases where a parent wishes to raise something without going through the school. I realize also that if, say, you have confirmed a permanent exclusion or dismissed a member of staff you may feel exposed to vengeful acts. I suggest these are matters governors should think about and discuss with their colleagues before they commit themselves to office.

Must we publish formal accounts?

 In our annual report to parents, which we want to make more friendly, do we have to give proper professional-style accounts or can we present information in everyday language and pictorially?

 Provided the information is comprehensive and clear you can present it in any way you like. The law says only that parents must be given information about the school budget and how it was spent. The danger is that in making it 'popular' governors over-simplify or omit important categories of spending. But I have seen many good reports – including some which have won TES awards – which have presented simple information illustrated with excellent pie-charts. Remember particularly to list gifts to the school – e.g. from the PTA – and how cash donations were spent. Remember that all funds used by schools from whatever source should be accounted for with the same care as public funds.

Some governors give brief indications of the budget breakdown in the report and provide full accounts at the meeting. This is only acceptable if the brief statement is in a form which satisfies legal requirements: otherwise the accounts should accompany the report. This is because the legal information must go to all parents, not just those who attend. It is also vital that those attending have the necessary material to base questions on, and time to consider them.

Why do teacher governors not play a full part?

   Our teacher governors have literally not said a word other than 'good evening' in the two years and three years respectively that they have served. I did dare to say to one when I was in the school that I would be interested to hear her views on a number of matters coming before governors and she replied that she and her colleague saw themselves as observers only. Could you say something about the role of teacher governors? I cannot believe that they were intended to be merely decorative.

   Indeed not. Yours is the most extreme case I have heard of, but many teacher governors do not play a full part, and among these are quite a few who are not encouraged to do so either by the LEA, or the head or some of their fellow governors. It is important to the effective working of the governing body that they are encouraged and supported, partly because we need the expert input from their knowledge and experience if we are to have good discussions about the school and its curriculum, partly because it is proper that the staff have a say through their representatives and a channel through which their concerns can be communicated.

Teacher governors are not delegates, i.e. they don't have to speak or vote as instructed by their colleagues, but they are representatives and they should (a) consult staff about matters coming up before governors; (b) bring staff concerns to governors; and (c) report back governors' decisions to the staff, provided they have not been classified as confidential.

All governors are intended to contribute equally to the work of the governing body and teacher governors no less than others are eligible to represent the governors on selection panels and serve on committees about pay, discipline and finance. The only restriction is the one which applies to all governors, namely they should not take part in a decision if they stand to gain personally from the outcome. Having said all this I have to add that in many schools teacher governors *are* discouraged from getting involved in what are regarded as 'sensitive' matters, and if they have problems playing a full part we should all try to help them to overcome those problems.

It is a difficult role. They may feel inhibited about discussing the school in the presence of 'outsiders' and their boss. They may be fearful about the consequences if they speak out of turn. They may feel conflicts of loyalty. Sometimes it may be necessary for the chair, or some governor or governors the head listens to, to seek his/her support in reassuring the teacher governors that taking part in open debate will not damage their careers, and that not only is their participation wanted but through them, that of the staff as a whole. If it falls to you to make this approach, do emphasize how important the teachers' expertise is to the quality of other governors' work and also how valuable it is for the staff to have the assurance that someone is being watchful for their interests and that they have a route to the governing body. (To be realistic, there will be a few heads who are not happy about anybody else speaking for the staff!)

There are other ways in which you can help teacher governors to make a fuller contribution. Remember to ask for their opinions specifically, or ask them to explain curriculum issues. Propose them for membership of committees and working parties, and suggest they serve on staff selection panels now and then. Get other teachers from the school to attend meetings on a regular basis in rotation to talk about their subject or class. Co-opt other teachers when appropriate onto committees or working parties. The teacher governors will feel more confident if other teachers get involved. Make sure you have a system for governors to spend some regular committed time in school sharing teachers' enthusiasms and getting to know more about how children learn.

When should teacher governors be excluded?

 A special meeting of governors was called to discuss 'staffing matters'. Staff were not told any more and teacher governors were excluded. The staffroom was abuzz with rumour and we all suffered real anxiety - for three weeks. We assumed the worst. Then we discovered it was about the head's desire to take early retirement. He did not wish his health, his attitude to the job, his package, or even his age, to be discussed in front of colleagues. Was this right?

 There was no justification for excluding teacher governors from such a meeting, quite apart from the unkindness of leaving staff to anxious speculation. The head's embarrassment may be understandable, but it is not the purpose of the rules to avoid embarrassment. Their object is to make sure that decisions are not skewed by personal interest, which in the case of teachers is defined as an interest 'greater than the generality of teachers'. In the coming years teacher governors will be part of many discussions which come too close for comfort to the affairs of colleagues, but I hope we shall grow up enough to see these as the issues in which teacher input is especially vital.

A teacher governor consults staff on a controversial issue

 We had a proposal on the agenda (referred by the personnel committee to the full governing body) to cut some non-teaching staff hours to save money. Our teacher governor discussed the item in the staff room before the governors' meeting and brought a protest from the staff which was tabled. He had not shown it to the head who felt aggrieved, and we all felt it was a breach of confidence to bring it up in the staffroom before governors had even discussed it. The staff had a case, namely that cutting non-teaching hours would mean an extra load on teachers and more time spent doing things other than teaching, but the way it was done seemed irregular.

 If the item had been classified as confidential by the committee referring it to the governing body, or if the agenda had suggested that it should be treated as confidential, I should agree. If not, however, I should say that the teacher governor was not only entitled but, as a representative, correct to consult colleagues. After all anyone dropping in from the street has a right to see governors' non-confidential papers, and we are talking here about people who are directly affected. The issue of tabling a paper without warning the head is another matter. Tabling papers is always a bad practice unless unavoidable, and doing so without informing the head is discourteous and liable to backfire.

When teacher governors disagree

I am just a teacher who is confused about the role of a teacher governor. We had a debate as a staff, in preparation for a governors' meeting, about exclusions. Our former head had strong principles about never using exclusion as a punishment: pupils might be sent home briefly to cool down, to take off dangerous shoes or ear-rings or bring in parents to discuss their behaviour, but punitive suspension, much less permanent exclusion, was not to be contemplated. He took the governors along with him, some I suspect reluctantly. Our new head wants to reverse the policy and have the governors spell out offences for which exclusion may be used. Most of us on the staff are loyal to the old head's policy but a small vocal minority feel that they want more support in dealing with bad behaviour.

We have one teacher governor in each camp. At the meeting they took opposite points of view. One in my opinion behaved quite properly in conveying the majority staff view against change. She, however, got a rocket from the head afterwards and was told it was not her job to speak for the staff. He clearly thought she should just support him. The other spoke up for the more punitive approach which actually was agreed by the governors, and he has had an equally hard time from the staff! I believe pupil behaviour has deteriorated as a direct consequence of a more authoritarian style and wanted that view strongly represented. Is that reasonable?

Teacher governors are not *delegates* and are not obliged to take staff instructions on how to vote. They are, however, representatives, and your head was quite wrong to say that it was not your colleagues' job to report staff views. They must listen and report as faithfully as they can, even if in a rare case they will want to take a different line which they sincerely believe is in the interests of the pupils. In my view your two colleagues should have stood together and jointly reported the balance of opinion in the staffroom, giving full weight to the majority's view and their reasons. They should then have followed their consciences, and the governor who was voting against majority staff opinion should have made this clear. Apart from anything else, it is essential that governors have the full benefit of different views, especially if the head is leaning on them a bit hard. I am troubled that such fundamental changes in behaviour guidelines had not been fully discussed in a forum of staff and governors before a formal meeting.

Teacher governors and confidentiality

You are always saying that most governors' business is not confidential. Yet as a teacher governor I have once again been warned by my head that if I tell my colleagues anything that has been decided at a governors' meeting I shall be disbarred from being a governor.

I am pleased to reassure you. Your head clearly does not realize how hard it is to get rid of a governor, even one whose fellow governors or electors are unanimously fed up with him or her! You are secure. He also does not seem to know that anyone can come in from the street and see governors' papers (apart from items the governors have deliberately classified as confidential, and these should be confined to matters concerning the private affairs of an individual), so it would be absurd to be more restrictive with people within the school. What you should not do is gossip about the detail of the meeting and how individuals voted. Just convey the majority view which you must be loyal to even if you did not agree.

Who speaks for 'the school'?

Can you please tell me where I stand as a head when a contentious matter is raised with governors? I feel that I speak for the school, and can over-rule the teacher governors' representations on behalf of the staff if no reconciliation is possible. The matter in question is a proposed change in the length of lesson period and as a result a small increase in the length of the school day. This is to accommodate the national curriculum requirements and at the same time keep a few choices traditionally important to our parents, ranging from economics to Latin. I have no doubt that the pupils' interests demand this.

Speaking for 'the school' is a difficult concept in current law. In a matter of policy the voice of the school is the majority vote of the governors. If you are a governor you have a vote, and the teacher governors each have the same right as you to contribute to the final decision, whether or not they follow the advice given to them by their colleagues. I have spoken many times of the difference between a delegate and a representative: briefly teacher governors must listen to colleagues, pass on their views to governors and report back, but in voting, after considering everything, follow what in conscience they see as the general interests of the school. I hope that your teachers will do this, and not merely voice sectional interests. In a few cases, of which changing the school day happens to be one (opting out is another), the matter does not end with the governors' vote but has to go to parents.

But of course you are more than one governor with one vote when it comes to advising the governors. You are also their chief professional adviser and are free to give them your own view of what the school's interests are. This is an influential role but it does not include the right to muzzle other views coming forward from those who work at the school which the governors as a whole must take into account along with others.

Governors and admission policies

I hope I may write as a PTA activist about an issue concerning our governors. The primary schools here are all full and our own school and several others are a little over-subscribed. The governors and LEA are apparently offering places at our school (because it is the largest and most central) to all the disappointed parents, and say they will provide a portable classroom if the numbers justify. We have not been told officially about it, and I only know because my third child is just due to start so I am in touch with other parents affected .

We cannot find out anything about this matter and have many questions. What happens if the extra numbers do not justify a full class so there is no extra teacher? What size will the reception classes be then? Will there be enough money for equipment and books? Our parent governors never communicate about anything they discuss and imply it is all hush-hush. I suspect governors have no real role at all and the hush-hush is just a cover-up.

This is a sad letter because it reveals that, in your school at least, having parent governors has done little to improve communication with parents. The first thing to say is that governors should certainly have been consulted about increasing the numbers, though in a county school they do not have anything to do with *individual* admissions. The second point is that all governors' papers are public documents and should be available in the school for anyone to read. There is provision for governors to classify items as confidential, but this is not intended for the concealment of policy matters, however controversial, but only for matters where individual privacy is involved. I would not regard taking additional numbers as suitable for classification. You and your fellow parents have a right to see any papers relating to the governors' discussion of this matter, and are entitled to ask your head where you can see them. But you should not be too hasty to condemn your governors (even though they are failing in their duty to keep you informed), because you are right in your suspicion that governors are sometimes not involved in matters that should legally come to them. Sometimes communication with parents is not made easy for them either.

You are also right to consider this matter a serious one. The short-term considerations you mention are vital. If the school has a delegated budget there will be enough money coming in with the additional children to safeguard their needs for books and equipment, so that is not a worry, but if there are not enough to pay for an extra teacher this income will either have to be robbed from some other heading or the classes will have to be bigger, and it is reasonable to want to know what size classes your children will be in. But long-term considerations are even more serious, not just for you but all parents, and you need to ask what will happen as this age group moves up the school, since apart from class space there will almost certainly be pressure on specialized accommodation and facilities, dining and recreation space, etc. If the school is to be significantly and permanently enlarged there should be public notices and opportunities for objections. Maybe some of the parents who have now been offered places will be delighted, but they and those who already have children at the school may not be too pleased about the general consequences.

I suggest that if you cannot get any information from your governors you get together with other affected or interested parents and ask for a meeting to discuss all the implications of taking extra numbers. The LEA should send someone who can give reassurances about the capital expenditure necessary now and in the future. Capital expenditure is outside the school budget.

Giving parents a chance to comment on the agenda

Our parent governor group has been talking about having a termly meeting with parents, timed just to precede full governing body meetings. The specific purpose would be to inform parents about the issues considered at governors' meetings and get their views on anything coming up at the next. We should of course encourage all governors to attend, not just parent governors, but I somehow think we will be the best attenders. The head says he does not object, neither do the other governors, and the PTA thinks it important too. What do you think? And should the head attend?

I think it is excellent and you are very lucky that everyone else concerned in your school agrees. Parents' rights to see agenda and minutes are rarely implemented in a way which gives them a real opportunity to contribute. Either the papers are so inaccessible as to deter any but the professional busybody, or the timing and amount of detail are not such as to make them a genuine form of communication, or parents are not reminded about their right to see them. I think it is also very good to make governors' work as a whole more visible in the school. It is a contribution to accountability, it encourages parents to think about issues that concern them, and it helps recruitment of new governors by making the governing body seem more real and relevant. As to the head's attendance, he must of course come if he wishes. If he is open and relaxed about controversy he would be an asset and you would be serving a further purpose in bringing parents' concerns to him. If he is more defensive his presence might inhibit discussion, but he does not sound as if he is. Three warnings: first do be sure it does not develop into a parent-governors-only occasion: I pick up a lot of resentment against parent governors who think they have a monopoly of communication, though I accept that they are the most natural and legitimate communicators. Second, do watch that it is not a negative occasion. I am sure you have ways of spreading the idea that words of praise and appreciation should be said out loud as well as more contentious things. Finally, do not be discouraged if attendances are not large at first. If the meetings are interesting it will soon get around.

Communicating with parents

 A relative who is a parent governor in another school is encouraged to communicate with parents through child post, even with a tear-off slip for a reply, is asked if she wants to put anything in the head's weekly newsletter, and has, with other parent governors, a session after school one day when parents can raise any points they wish. In contrast I am told that as a parent governor it is not my job to find out parents' opinions or divulge governors' business to them and I have been flatly refused permission to have a 'surgery'.

 Yes. Same law, same government, same LEA, different head. One more instance of how much influence heads have. If you want to quote me on whether parents have a representative role, listening, bringing parent concerns to the proper quarter, reporting back (provided you scrupulously respect confidential items, are 100% accurate and do not report meetings at the personal gossip level but only convey majority decisions) – well, here I am saying it for about the hundredth time. You do have that role. But I don't think it is going to help you much. One sad lesson we learn daily is that you can only start from where you are, not where your sister or cousin is, and must concentrate on moving forward at a pace your situation can cope with without strain. That is inevitable in an evolving system which can only evolve through goodwill. You can't insist on having a surgery on school premises (and having one elsewhere would be confrontational) and I don't advocate calling it a 'surgery' anyway if there is resistance, because it suggests the unsupervised encouragement to complain, which is what heads fear. I think you should see your first steps as the chance to be present and identified at all meetings well supported by parents, and possibly to ask the head nicely to look at a piece you have written reporting some matter of interest to parents for possible inclusion in *her* newsletter or the PTA newsletter. If you take it steadily you will win her trust in time, especially if you are in general supportive and pleasant and always remember to pass on any nice things parents say or any positive points of your own.

Can a parent governor discuss reorganizing her child's class?

 The head asked me to leave the meeting because they were going to discuss the pros and cons of converting four junior classes into three and my child is in the juniors. Should I have been asked to leave?

 Certainly not. All governors are under a constraint not to take part in decisions from which they might individually benefit, but many parents are involved in the kind of change you were discussing and it seems absurd to carry the 'special interest' rule so far. Perhaps the head was afraid you would gossip about the proposal and cause alarm. Two things to say about that. First, I do not see it as an item which should be made confidential. Second, it is insulting to suggest that parent governors are more inclined to gossip than others.

In any case it is not the head who decides but the governors as a whole. Either head or chair may remind them of the rules but they decide how to apply them.

How much to report back

 How much of the discussion on a non-confidential item can be reported by a governor, say a parent governor or teacher governor, both of whom have, you say, a right to report back to those they represent? I was not very pleased as chair to find out that a governor had reported how everybody voted on the issue of grant-maintained status, that the head had been made to look foolish by a governor who was a lawyer on a point of law which she had got wrong, and that the local contractor submitting the lowest tender for a school contract was rejected because of a bad reputation.

 This governor is behaving very improperly. The decisions on non-confidential items can certainly be reported. For example: 'the governors decided by a majority of seven to five to go to ballot on GMS'; 'it was pointed out that the law did not permit co-opted governors to vote on future co-options'; 'after discussion of the tenders submitted for the new bicycle sheds it was agreed to accept that of Messrs Bildem and Runn'. The main arguments advanced could also be reported without names. But it is not only discourteous but a breach of governors' corporate loyalty to gossip about the detail of debate and voting or to put any colleague in a bad light. In the case of the contractor it could be slanderous.

You should take the first opportunity to remind governors of these points.

Getting parent governors who are genuinely representative

 I am head of a primary school serving a mixed area. I get very annoyed with our parent governors (fairly new) who come from the more prosperous section of our community and make no attempt to 'represent' the majority, many of whose children frankly have a poor start in life and need all our support. Everything they say or advocate is slanted towards the needs of the more fortunate, they make no effort to contact parents other than those they meet socially, and often they seem thoughtless if not actually uncaring about the school's problems. How can I promote a more responsible attitude?

I often get grumbles about parent governors whose starting point is their experience with their own children, though not always with this social slant. I know how trying it is but I always remind myself that all direct experience is valid and we waited a long time to have it represented in school government at all. What we have to do is broaden it.

Your long-term problem is to get a balance of governors which more properly reflects your community. There is no substitute for this. I am sure you do everything you can to encourage parents from the majority group to stand for election and to encourage widespread participation in voting as well. It is a long-term project which will be helped, I realize, by a more caring attitude on the governing body you have, so you have to pursue the two aims at once. I am sure that you also do everything you can to increase the confidence of parents who have not had much success in life, to ease their contacts with the school and to lose no opportunity to say that being a school governor is a job intended for any parent who cares about education, and requires no special qualifications. Try to identify some leaders.

To return to the parent governors you have, point their eyes always in the direction of what they would otherwise miss. Use their visits to the school and any work-sharing on your governing body to enlarge their experience. Could your chair not ensure that they get a personal responsibility for some area of work which will broaden their interests and sympathies? Can you encourage them in various ways to accept a more representative role, give them all possible help to communicate and sound out parental feelings about school policies? You, as a professional, must be an expert at communicating high expectations of people, without instructing, exhorting, preaching, without even words. You probably use these skills more often with your staff than your governors. See if you can manage to convey, without saying so, your expectation that they will try to represent all parents. Remember that in time other governors will influence them too.

Dealing with parents' concerns

 I know you get this question often, but how can I convince our head that it is not threatening if parents come to me as their governor about little concerns? Why is she so touchy about it? I always encourage parents to go to the teacher or the head, and if they will not, I offer to take up the point for them. I do not want to take over anybody's role, but parents do find it easy to approach somebody they see at the gate, as you have said, and they believe that I am there to help them. The head says it is not my job to 'collect complaints' and that it is no more a parent governor's role to communicate than other governors.

 I am on your side of course. Parent governors do have a special duty to listen and try to facilitate and smooth parents' contact with the school. As long as you keep encouraging them to feel easier about going into school, never bypass the head, never use governors' meetings to bring up a string of unrelated parents' complaints, and remember to pass on the nice things people say about the school, you are behaving correctly.

Why is the head touchy, you say? It is the fear of any communication which excludes her, basically I think, and we have to understand that if a person has always been at the centre of all the communication in and out, it is quite hard for her to get used to the idea that somebody who does not work for her, is not under her control, has not the kind of accountability that a staff member has, might be the first point of contact. If you go on behaving responsibly and courteously she will come to trust you. Try to explain that many parents do fear schools, fear that their worry might be too trivial or that they have got it all wrong, and assure her that you will do nothing but seek her guidance on any matter brought to you in this way. Actually many schools which fuss about parent governors getting queries from parents are often not as open as they think they are, and might do better if they had a set time when parents knew there was a member of staff available for personal worries, however small. Try to get across the point that it is far healthier for concerns to come through you than not to come out at all, or be the subject of school gate gossip and misunderstanding.

Can a parent governor be on a disciplinary panel?

 Unfortunately we have had to embark on a disciplinary action against a teacher. My governing body is setting up a committee for this and I was proposed with a great deal of support to be a member. I am a parent governor, and I hope my colleagues wanted me to be involved because they thought I would be capable and fair, and also perhaps because I was a personnel officer before I had my family. Even the teacher governors were anxious for me to be involved. The head, however, said that it was not proper for a parent from the school to be discussing a teacher and that it would be most unfortunate if the proceedings were to be relayed to the 'school gate committee'. I don't know the meaning of this reference: we have no gossip at the gate as far as I know and I have always been scrupulous about keeping matters concerning individuals to myself. I would be wouldn't I with my background?

 Of course you would, and I can say without hesitation that your head is totally in the wrong on this. First, it is not for the head to say who should be on committees or to produce his own interpretation of the rules. Both the delegation of functions and the final judgement on what is proper belong to governors as a body. In any case your service on this committee does not break any rules: all governors are equal in their right to participate, with the single proviso – which applies to all governors equally – that if a governor stands to profit as an individual from the outcome of a decision, he/she should not take part.

I find it particularly upsetting when parent governors are singled out for veiled suggestions that they might gossip about confidential matters, or there is a suggestion that there is something improper about a parent governor discussing the competence or behaviour of a teacher. I would not claim that there are no parent governors who misbehave sometimes, like other governors. But when people have accepted public office there is no alternative to assuming that they will be trustworthy.

Governors and the latest fashion crazes

   Parents are complaining to us about a proposed new rule banning a certain footwear fashion and insisting on 'conventional design' shoes. We narrowly avoided banning famous name trainers, which for years led to regular thefts of cash to buy them, but at least trainers were easier to define! The rule takes effect after half-term. Parents complain they can't buy new shoes just like that.

   I understand the desire to do something about these crazes, but changes in school dress should be fully discussed with parents and enough warning given for existing clothes to be outgrown. Then you risk banning a fashion nobody would be seen dead in by the time it becomes a rule! Watch out for the return of winkle-pickers or grandfathers' old cardigans with gravy stains and holes in. (I well remember our own grandfather's bewilderment when he was offered a brand new cardigan bought from Saturday earnings in exchange for such coveted relics.) Meanwhile all those liberal schools with their student-designed red sweat shirts risk having blazers becoming all the rage. You can't win. I am not going to get into a discussion on uniform, since such discussions already cost a fortune in caretakers' overtime, but schools *must* take governors with them in something which concerns parents so much, and governors in turn can't ignore parents' feelings, especially when there is no health or safety reason for an expensive decision.

A disruptive parent at the annual parents' meeting

   For the second year running our annual meeting with parents has been disrupted by one parent who constantly interrupts and shouts other people down. His aggressive and intimidating behaviour has upset other parents, several of whom left the meeting early in dismay. It is not all that easy to attract parents anyway, so what can we do to ensure an orderly meeting? Do governors have powers to exclude one parent for the protection of others?

No, I think not. Indeed I would say every parent has a legal right to attend the meeting, though I sympathize with your concern. I assume your chair did everything possible to run the meeting in an orderly way without effect. It does not sound as if the obvious disapproval of fellow parents is effective either, which suggests to me either that this person has a massive grievance or frustration associated with the school or an overwhelming need to make a personal impact. Either way can you not devise some way of defusing him outside the meeting? If he has indicated any specific subject of concern, could not you invite him to part of a governing body meeting some time before the next annual event to tell governors what is on his mind, so that you can, if you think it is a valid point, address it in the report? Or would your parent governors be willing to seek him out and ask, in view of his comments at meetings, whether there is anything he would like to bring to their notice? I would not rule out the possibility that he does have some serious point to make but finds it hard to make it in an acceptable way. In these cases it is often helpful to invite people to write their concern down – another possible defusing technique.

Holding governors to account for budget decisions

A recent case reported in the press has prompted me to write, as a parent, about our governors' actions. Ours is a large comprehensive where parents are making huge efforts to raise funds to replace a clapped out minibus. There has been a lot of anger about governors having £12,000 earmarked as a contingency fund which in all probability will not be spent and will be lost to the school. We have asked for a justification of this and have not had a satisfactory reply, so we are also thinking of passing a vote of no confidence and calling for the removal of our governors. Comments please.

It is not that easy to remove governors. The LEA could suspend a governing body's budget responsibility if they had grossly mismanaged the school's financial affairs, but it is inconceivable that this would be considered in the circumstances you mention. In a large comprehensive we are probably talking about a budget of upwards of £2 million, and a contingency fund of £12,000 (well under 1%) does not seem unduly large, especially in the early days of LMS when there must be a lot of guesswork as well as natural fear of disasters. The governors would be more likely to earn the charge of irresponsibility if they cut it too fine. The money will not be lost to the school but will be carried over.

Although parents cannot remove their governors, they are entitled to some accountability about the use of funds. The annual report must give budget information and the annual meeting affords an opportunity to question it, but in any case sensible governors should be prepared to justify their action on such an important matter at any time. If parents think the governors should make provision in the budget for replacing the minibus, they are entitled to say so and have a reasoned reply. The best thing would be to try to talk to your parent governors about the poor communication which seems to exist in your school and impress upon them that they must use their influence to get parents listened to. It is bad for everybody if parents' feelings about fund-raising become so sour.

A parent governors' surgery

I am a new parent governor and with the parent group would like to establish a surgery for parents to bring matters to us. The head seems very opposed to this and will not allow us space or publicize it. Are we entitled to go ahead, and do you agree with such a system?

Technically nobody can stop you meeting somewhere as a group to give parents a chance to bring up matters which concern them, but without the head's co-operation you cannot organize it within the school, and I think it is disastrous to over-ride the head's feelings anyway. Again technically it is true that if the *governing body* decided that it should happen as a matter of policy, the head could not prevent it, but that is so unlikely in the circumstances that it is scarcely a realistic option.

I am fully in favour of parents feeling that they can approach parent governors with their concerns, and believe that schools should encourage governors to attend, and be identified at, all parent gatherings. They should indeed make it easy for parent governors to listen and act as a bridge with the school. The trouble is that if you call it a 'surgery' it may seem as if you are encouraging complaints. You do not go to the doctor to say how well you feel. Many heads react against it for that reason, though

I have heard of a few schools where they have a regular session for parents and parent governors with the head's support and some even call it a surgery.

This again underlines what I often say, that we must all start from where we are. Given the opposition I should if I were you proceed more tactfully, make sure that you attend all meetings for parents, keep in close touch with the parents' association, if any, listen wherever you can. You may be able to progress to a parent governors' item in the school or parents' newsletter and perhaps a coffee or tea hour for other parents to meet their parent governors socially. Opposition to governors getting involved in communication in their own right is often based on fear, and you must be careful you do not increase that fear. One thing you must not compromise on, however, is the right of parents to approach you if they have a concern they feel diffident about going to the school with. It is a proper role for parent governors to help less confident parents with access to the school, provided they always work with the head and on no account spring things on him/her at the governors' meetings.

Should parent governors listen to parents' complaints?

 You often advise parent governors in your various writings on how to deal with worries, problems, even complaints, brought to them by parents. I always understood that all governors once appointed had the same responsibilities - to the school not their interest group - and that it was no more parent governors' job to communicate with and deal with enquiries from parents than any other governor. As a head I am not comfortable with individual concerns being brought to a governor rather than the school, and consider that parent governors should refuse to listen to these complaints and refer parents to me.

 I agree that all governors have the same responsibilities for the school and that in the end these take precedence over the interests of the group they represent. I would also say that the governing body as a whole ought to be watchful of the school's communication with parents and be ready to raise difficulties or suggest improvements.

I do *not* agree, nor is there any basis in law or regulations for claiming, that governors have no individual responsibility towards the group that elected them: the representative role (which is different from a delegate role) is implicit in the act of election. I see it as parent governors' special duty to listen to parents, bring their views to governors, and keep them in touch with parts of governors' work which specially concern them.

Having said that, I always advise parent governors to steer individual concerns (as distinct from widespread ones which might need a place on the agenda) to the school if possible. I also say that if the parent concerned is timid, the governor might accompany him/her, and if very timid, see the head on his/her behalf. I add that it is a good idea for parent governors to discuss with head teachers from time to time how parental access might be improved, and I never fail to warn governors that they must not in any circumstances bypass the head in any action or response to complaint. I believe it is unrealistic to expect all parents to feel confident about approaching the school themselves, and that it is natural that they should turn to a parent governor. Often they are afraid their worry might be considered too trivial to take up with the school. Or they fear they may have got the wrong end of the stick and do not want to look silly. For this reason I favour schools advertising a special time in the week when there will be someone available to deal with minor matters, always making it clear that major or urgent problems can be brought to school at any time. Looked at positively, the parent governor's role can be seen as an asset to a head, a ready insight into parents' concerns and an early warning system.

Parent governors and confidential information

 As a head I feel very uneasy about parent governors having access to private information about our own teachers from application forms, references, etc. when they take part in selection panels. It is even more worrying when they are on committees dealing with teachers' pay, promotion and discipline. Recently we had to take disciplinary action against one of our teachers, and the governors put a parent governor on the committee looking into the matter. We know parents chatter at the gate and information might get to a parent with children in these teachers' classes. Can't we exclude them?

 Governors' have equal rights and responsibilities. The only legal restriction on the participation of any governor relates to pecuniary interest or, in the case of disciplinary matters, direct involvement in the incidents concerned. The purpose is to prevent decisions being made by people who cannot be seen to be objective because of a direct personal involvement. It is not to avoid embarrassment or to prevent gossip. Governors must always be reminded of the need to keep their counsel on matters which affect the private lives of teachers or pupils, but I think many parent governors would be very hurt at the suggestion that they are less trustworthy than others. The only assumption on which public bodies can work is that every member merits trust.

7 Meetings and committees

The meeting is the thing

However well governors communicate, inform and involve themselves, and represent the school in the community, it is the decisions they make together which matter most. Only the decisions made at quorate, properly convened and conducted meetings have any validity. That sounds very obvious, but there are plenty of examples in this book of decisions made or thought to be made by governors in very much more casual ways.

Rules are good for you

The rules about meetings, which you will find in your *Governors' Guide to the Law*, are not just dry bureaucracy. They are designed to ensure that all governors share responsibility; that decisions are not made by too few people; that meetings are conducted in a fair and orderly way; that when power is delegated it is done consciously, seriously and precisely; and that decisions are not influenced by anyone who profits from them.

Confidentiality

Governors' business is intended to be public as far as possible, and all governors' papers, unless *they* themselves (not the head, chair or clerk) classify them confidential, are public documents. Confidentiality should not be over-used: it is clear that the government intended it to be used only to protect individual privacy. All other governors' papers can be read on request, not just by parents and staff (to whom they should be readily accessible) but also by any member of the public.

Quorum

This is the minimum number of governors who have to be present to make decisions legal. For most tasks it is one-third, but for certain particularly vital things (e.g., co-opting colleagues or delegating responsibility) it is two-thirds. Co-opted governors cannot vote in future co-options (except in grant-maintained schools).

Chair and vice chair

The chair and vice chair may not be employees of the school, and this restriction applies also to committees which have delegated powers. Committees or working parties which need their decisions endorsed by the whole governing body are exempt from any restriction on who takes the chair: it could be a teacher in a working party on the curriculum, for instance, if that is what all governors wish, since curriculum responsibility cannot be delegated. The chair has no automatic right to make decisions on behalf of governors except in a serious emergency: otherwise any action he/she takes must be on the governing body's instructions.

Committees

Committees are a good idea (if not overdone) since they enable more individuals to participate confidently, allow for issues to be discussed in more detail, and save time at governors' meetings (*caution*: be careful they do save time: do not re-run the same discussions).

Delegation

Delegation to committees is possible for a few tasks, illegal for many, and essential for a few. *Your Guide to the Law* gives a full list. Among responsibilities you can legally delegate for example are finance, routine care of the premises, and appointments (except that head teacher appointments must be ratified by the governing body). You cannot delegate *decisions*(though useful preparatory work can be done by small groups of course) on a long list of responsibilities, which include the curriculum, with religious education and worship and sex education underlined; on admissions policy; on co-options; on approving the annual report to parents, behaviour guidelines or charging policy; on any major changes in the character of the school (going to ballot on grant-maintained status for instance); and school holiday dates.

You *must* have subcommittees for any function of governors which might lead to an appeal, so that some governors are available to come unprejudiced to an appeal. These include pay, teacher grievance and discipline and pupil exclusion.

Governors decide the terms of reference of committees. They may if they wish elect the chair of a committee themselves, or leave it to the committee to elect its own chair.

Decisions

Decisions are by *majority vote*, with the chair having a casting vote in the event of a tie. Decisions on going to ballot on grant-maintained status must be by secret ballot. Otherwise governors decide themselves on open or secret voting, subject to anything different in their own local articles.

Rescinding a decision

If governors at a meeting *rescind* a previous decision, it must have been clear from the agenda that this was to be discussed.

Special interest

A governor should be *excluded* from a decision if *he/she* personally might profit from the outcome, e.g. gain a contract, open up a promotion opportunity, favour or unduly blame a pupil being excluded (this could apply to a parent or the teacher mainly involved in the incidents). The head should never be present for any governors' decision on reinstating or permanently excluding a pupil, and this decision cannot be delegated to an individual, only a group of at least three.

Better meetings

The reasons for all these requirements for a *legal* meeting should be clear. But this is only a beginning. What makes it a *good* meeting? The first requirement is that it should make, and have recorded, clear decisions, not just clear on what was decided but also on who was responsible for the next action, by when and reporting to whom. The discussion should be relevant and as brief as the subject allows, but without curtailing contributions or leaving anyone feeling aggrieved – a task for a really good chair.

It may be helpful to set time limits for each item to ensure that time is left for major items and not squandered. If the chair does this it is wise to seek governors' prior approval to the plan for the meeting: if they feel responsible for it they are less likely to be offended if their contribution is curtailed.

Remember always that it is the governing body's meeting. They decide as a group what to discuss, what to make confidential, how to manage the business, whom to elect to committees or selection panels, how to apply the rules, what visitors to invite. They can even ask to agree the wording of the minutes on a particular item on the spot if it is critical. They must be clear about this.

Please read this introduction in conjunction with Chapter 8. The relationship between meeting rules and holding tight to shared responsibility is close, and the border area between legal requirements and good team-building full of overlap.

Who decides what is confidential?

    Parents and staff at our school are troubled by the large amount of governors' business apparently recorded as confidential. This means there is little they can report back. Are not governors accountable, to parents especially, for decisions? Who has the right to decide what may and may not be made public and on what grounds? Can minutes already classed as confidential be 'de-regulated'? If so whom should we approach?

    This is a good example of how easy it is for individuals or groups, if they are so motivated, to take advantage of governors' lack of information and usurp the powers which the governing body holds. I have no idea who it is in your case: sometimes it is the LEA, sometimes the head, occasionally the chair or clerk, but often an individual governor or small group who follow their own agenda unchallenged. Confidentiality can be a powerful weapon for those who seek power.

I can assure you with no doubt at all that it is the governing body as a whole and nobody else who has the right to classify information as confidential, and if the governors have not so voted, the item is *not* confidential. The clerk, chair or head may occasionally need to alert governors to the delicacy of a particular item and remind them that they must make a decision, but the decision itself is for you and your colleagues.

I can also assure you that the intention of the law is that governors should be accountable to parents and staff, that most governors' business should be open, and that confidentiality should be kept to the bare minimum. The wording of the regulations makes it clear that in the main confidential items will be those where it is necessary to protect the privacy of an individual, a pupil, parent, teacher or other person. There may be other occasional cases where, at the governors' discretion, an item may be classified – perhaps a planning, contract or business issue where someone outside the school might be able to extract a personal advantage from advance knowledge. But in general the fact that a matter is controversial or embarrassing is not sufficient reason for classifying it.

The minutes of a meeting should be within the governors' control, not just in matters of classification but also in what is minuted, and occasionally with particularly difficult items the form of words to be used, which can be agreed at the meeting. There is no reason why governors, if they are all of one mind, should not retrospectively 'de-classify' items from past minutes.

If you want an assurance from the Department for Education that confidentiality is indeed within your control I am sure they will be happy to give you one. You may find that this letter is sufficient. Your colleagues will surely take seriously the fact that they are frustrating the *intention* of the law by keeping so much under wraps.

But where does it say?

 As an inexperienced governor I often have a feeling that decisions are not being made properly. We are too casual, we assume agreement too easily when some do not have the confidence to contest a point, and sometimes are told we cannot do this or must do the other, without most of us knowing whether that is correct or not. Sometimes I am pretty sure that the advice is not right, and does not seem to square with openness or fairness. But because I don't have chapter and verse I am afraid of looking silly or being branded a nit-picker.

 You describe a very familiar problem now that many governing bodies do not have an authoritative person from the LEA at meetings and have to be responsible for their own rule-keeping. We must become familiar with the working rules as soon as we can and encourage colleagues to do the same. Use your DFE *Guide to the Law* and see the reference to the Northamptonshire publication *Working Together* on page 219. Ask for chapter and verse to be given if anyone claims to know it all. You can be courteous, genuinely seeking to learn. Intentionally or not, powerful people take advantage of those who are not sure where they stand. We must not let this happen. And agreement should never be assumed: it is far better to be formal and ask around the table what individuals think than let them be too timid to express a view.

Can governors be prevented from seeing letters addressed to them?

 Is there any requirement on the chair or head to acquaint governors with letters they have received when specifically asked to do so? When I left the school I was teaching in until recently, there were certain important points I wanted to bring to governors' attention, not personal matters but relevant to the well-being of my department and certainly within governors' sphere of responsibility. I understand that it was simply reported that the letter had been received and that the head would deal with it.

 There is nothing in education law or regulations requiring all governors to see letters addressed to them as a body, but I should regard it as very bad behaviour for the chair of any committee to suppress such a letter when specifically asked to share it. In the nature of things there is nothing governors can do if they do not know this is happening, but when they discuss in general – as they should – how they are going to organize their paperwork, they might make it clear that they do wish to see all correspondence which comes to the school for their attention. All you can do is to copy your comments to every governor yourself – their names will be in your school brochure or your governors' last annual report to parents. You can send them either through the school or the LEA for forwarding. Alternatively you might ask the teacher governors to raise the issue if they are brave enough.

Sewing up the committees

 Our outgoing chairman has circulated a paper for the first meeting of the school year setting out the new committees and the core membership. It will not, of course, include any new governors. It also seems to assume we re-elect the chairman, (which after this I am not so keen on!). He has drawn this up with the head. The head and chairman are on every committee and the chairman chairs policy and finance. The head is shown as chairman of the staff and pupil discipline committee (which has no parent or teacher governor on it), and a deputy head responsible for curriculum who is not even a governor is shown as chair of the

curriculum committee. Some governors do not appear. (Troublemakers? If so, I am one.) Last year it was more or less what you would approve of, I think, so this seems like a plan to tighten up control. We feel stunned by it – is it legal, proper? Please advise.

 Your outgoing chair while he remains a governor can make any suggestions he likes. So can the head or you or any other governor still in office. But they can be no more than suggestions. The only legal decisions about setting up committees and their membership are those made co-operatively by a quorate meeting of your governing body, so do not fall for this high-handed and improper attempt to usurp the role of the governors as a whole. Your chair is presuming that he will be re-elected or else cashing in on what remains of his authority, but in fact decisions made by committees with delegated powers can be overturned (and already have been in two cases, one by the courts and one by the Secretary of State for Wales) on the ground that their membership was not properly agreed by the whole governing body.

You should at your meeting discuss the tasks to be covered and the structure you need to carry them out. You should all participate in deciding on the membership according to interest and aptitude but it is also a good principle to share membership of important committees fairly across interest groups. It is up to you as a governing body to decide who shall chair various committees, or alternatively you can if you wish decide to leave it to the committee to elect its own chair. But no employee of the school can legally chair a committee with delegated powers, so it would be improper for instance for the head to chair Finance if that committee has such powers. This doesn't apply to the deputy chairing a curriculum working party, since curriculum decisions can't be delegated, but it is for the governors or the working party itself to co-opt the deputy (in itself a good idea) and to elect the chair. It *is* illegal for the head to chair a committee dealing with staff and pupil discipline, which must in the nature of things have delegated powers, and the head may not legally even be a member of a group which decides whether or not to reinstate an excluded pupil. He/she must also withdraw from any appeal in a disciplinary case involving either teacher or pupil where he/she has been a participant in the original disciplinary action. The head does, however, have the right to be present at any other committee meeting, whether or not a member, and even if not a governor, though of course only governor heads may vote. These rules are contained in Statutory Instrument No. 1503 1989.

I hope that your governing body will resist this attempt to undermine its role and that you will also discuss, before you elect a chair, the kind of relationship you want between the chosen person and the rest of you. This is your one chance to change practices which have not proved acceptable.

Can governors set up a committee on charges for school trips?

 Can we set up a committee to make decisions about changes in our school's arrangements for charging for trips, etc.? Some problems have arisen with the policy we originally established and it needs another look, preferably with a bit more time than we normally have for extra items on our agenda.

 You cannot set up a committee to 'make decisions' on charging policy because it is one of the things governors may not delegate. But there is no reason why you should not set up an informal working party, to look at the issues and bring them to the governing body with options and arguments clearly set out. This should save time in making the decision. It is a very important issue and you are right to want to allow time for proper consideration.

Setting up a pay committee

 Our chairman decided during the holiday that we need a committee to deal with teachers' discretionary pay decisions. He has asked the vice-chairman and another co-opted governor who is a personnel officer in a local firm to serve with him and said that the head should also attend. Is it right that important decisions should be made by such a small group and that the head should be there?

 There are at least five questions here! Simplest first: yes it is right that a committee should be set up to deal with pay and indeed any issues (like pupil exclusions and teacher discipline) which may lead to appeals, grievance procedures, etc. This is so that there is no question of any appeal being determined by the people who made the decision appealed against. Looking ahead to that eventuality I would say it is better if either the chair *or* vice-chair serves.

Second, heads have a legal right to be present at any committee of governors, subject to the usual rules (i.e., they must withdraw when direct personal interest arises), *except* that they may not serve on a committee considering the re-instatement of an excluded pupil. I would personally advocate making the head a member of the pay committee and I should be happier if there were a teacher governor also (again subject to the rules on direct interest).

Now for the even more important issues. It is desirable that before any committee is set up to deal with pay (perhaps any subject) the governors as a whole discuss the general principles/criteria to be applied to decisions. The chances of trouble arising from any decision on the detail are greatly lessened, and the treatment of grievances if they arise enormously helped, by having clear and consistent policies, especially when staff governors contribute freely.

The way in which your chair has dealt with the setting up of a committee is totally irregular. Governors who propose to delegate any power must do so corporately at a full meeting, and a special quorum of two-thirds is necessary. They must set out clearly the terms of reference of the committee and elect its members. Otherwise, the decisions of the 'committee' are not legal. You may remember a case where an appointment was challenged because, among other irregularities, the chair nominated one of the panel without discussion by other governors. There is also a case where the Secretary of State for Wales ruled a decision on exclusion of pupils irregular because the chair had appointed the relevant committee. Please ensure that this is brought to your chair's notice: you could be in serious trouble otherwise.

Can the head be clerk?

 Is a head teacher allowed to be clerk to the governing body? Our head has proposed that he should take on the role, and says it would save us money as he could use the facilities of the school and would not expect any payment. We have deferred a decision to await your advice.

I can find no legal objection to a head teacher becoming clerk, provided this is the free will of the governing body, whose decision it is. I don't think it is at all desirable, since the head inevitably enjoys a position of great respect with his governing body which ill accords with the idea of being their servant as clerk. Because of the authority of the head it would also be difficult for the average governor to challenge an action or ruling by the head acting as clerk. It is important that governors feel that the clerk is there to give effect to their wishes and that they should feel free to express them.

I should not pay too much attention to the money question since, in my experience, the allowance for clerking is meagre. It does not make any difference that school facilities are used, since secretarial time, stationery, telephone calls, postage, photocopying, all come out of the school's budget, even if it is a different pocket. Many schools are generous with these facilities anyway if they have a volunteer clerk.

Can the LEA control our agenda?

 We are unhappy about the way a decision was made in the school. I need not go into detail, but it was a case of the head making a decision that we consider should legally have come to governors. We have asked for a special meeting to raise the matter but our LEA has refused to accept this as an agenda item. It is a long tradition in our county that the ruling party is very protective of teachers, working closely with their professional associations. This has its good side but it goes too far. Can they censor our business in this way?

 In general no. I find that some LEAs are living in the past and contesting decisions which are not now theirs to contest. Governors have control of their own business and cannot be prevented from holding a meeting or putting what they wish on the agenda. The LEA are entitled to advise if they think governors are acting unwisely, especially in personnel matters where governors' decisions will only be backed (in a financial sense) by the LEA if the LEA has supported them. If, for instance, the governors dismissed a teacher against LEA advice, and the teacher subsequently was awarded compensation by an industrial tribunal, the school would pick up the bill. If the LEA supported the governors' action they would pay any costs.

Powers of the chair

 What sort of decisions is it proper for a chairperson to make between meetings? Should they always be reported back at a governors' meeting?

 The chair has no automatic authority at all to make *decisions* on behalf of the governing body except in a dire emergency – like a fire – when there is no time even to call a special meeting. *Action* taken following a *governors'* decision (e.g., signing a letter conveying the outcome of a hearing in a permanent exclusion case, or informing the residents' association that the governors have agreed to plant some trees to screen the new bicycle sheds), should always be briefly reported at the next meeting.

Apart from asking the chair to carry out some action which they have agreed upon, governors may of course *delegate* a particular decision to the chair. It must be formally recorded and it must be a decision which it is proper to delegate – which *excludes* among other things any decisions on the curriculum, religious education and worship, sex education, admissions, opting out. A decision on whether to reinstate a permanently excluded pupil can never be delegated to an individual, only a committee. The most common decisions to delegate are on finance and teacher appointments. A finance committee which itself has delegated powers may for instance agree that the chair can authorize expenditure up to a certain sum being transferred from one budget head to another. On teacher appointments a governing body may legally decide that they will always be represented by the chair or another governor nominated by him/her. I do not think this is ideal practice but it is quite common.

Some chairs undoubtedly do take decisions alone – about money, personnel issues, curriculum changes, discipline - which are not legal, and it is dangerous as well as interfering with governors' proper role. A lot of planning and foresight is necessary to avoid this, and governors need to look ahead much more to ensure that they make or delegate decisions on matters on which action must take place before they meet again. 'So what do I do?' a chairperson might well ask, 'apart from running the meeting efficiently, bringing out the best in my team and being a mouthpiece? I am in the school a couple of times a week, there always seems plenty to discuss and give opinions on, and the head relies on me.' The relationship is certainly important: heads often feel isolated and want a sympathetic ear. They often want someone to reassure them about some decision or action which they are legally quite entitled to take themselves, e.g. suspending a teacher pending an enquiry into some irregularity or excluding a pupil for a week. They may want to change some aspect of the school's internal organization, like swopping a teacher to another class or using space differently. Occasionally some such routine action may be such as to ruffle staff feathers or upset parents, and having moral back-up is helpful even if it is not formal.

There is no harm in being a sounding board in a matter which is not for governors' formal decision anyway, as long as one remembers that in an issue which may lead to a grievance or discipline case, prior involvement may exclude the governor concerned from any formal role later.

Can a head take the chair in an exclusion appeal?

 Our head teacher takes the chair when the governors are deciding whether or not to confirm a permanent exclusion of a pupil. This seems unfair. Advice please.

 It certainly is not right. It makes nonsense of a quasi-judicial procedure relating to the head teacher's proposed action. It is also on at least three counts illegal. First, under Regulations 9(5) and 26(7) of the Education (School Governing Bodies) Regulations 1989 (SI 1503) no employee of the school may be chair of a committee with delegated powers. Second, a committee to decide the permanent fate of an excluded pupil must include at least three governors *'none of whom shall be the head teacher'* –Regulation 26(6). Finally, under paragraph 5(d) of the Schedule to the Regulations a head teacher who has been involved in a disciplinary action against a pupil or a teacher must withdraw from any meeting where that action is being appealed against.

Can a head chair the finance committee?

 Can the head teacher be a member of the budget committee and is he eligible to be chairman? Ours has taken it for granted that he will do both, and some of us think it is not right that he should have so much influence over finance.

 A head who is a governor may be appointed to any committee (the only exception being one deciding whether to reinstate an excluded pupil). However, the decision is the governors' and right to membership should not be assumed. In any case the head (whether or not a governor) has the right to attend any meeting, other than one hearing an appeal against disciplinary action (teacher or pupil) where he/she has been a participant in the events leading to the action.

No employee of a school may be chair of the governing body itself, and the same rule applies to any committee to which governors have delegated power. This prohibition does not apply to other subgroups of governors, that is working parties without delegated powers: in these cases the governors agree on their own rules.

Do governors' committee papers have to be open to the public?

 Do committee minutes have to be available to the public as well as governors' full meeting minutes?

 I imagine that you submit some sort of written report or minutes and supporting papers from all committees and working parties to the full governing body. These, along with other governors' papers not classified as confidential, can be seen by the public on request. In addition, any unclassified papers from a committee with delegated powers are public documents in their own right. You must in short be prepared for any governors' papers to be open unless you classify all or part as confidential. Confidential matter will not be included in the papers available to the public. But don't overdo confidentiality. It is normally only appropriate for matters affecting individual privacy.

Frequency of meetings

 Some of us have been talking in the holidays about the way we work together, and feel that we need more than one meeting a term. We meet too infrequently for any real team-building and the things we discuss are often remote . Can we insist on another meeting?

 You can organize your business in any way a majority want, provided you meet a minimum of once a term. I am always saying how important the first meeting of the year is in improving our work (see also pages 181-2). This is your chance to raise the question of frequency, and also perhaps your effectiveness more generally, since if you have no committees either I cannot imagine that you are even fulfilling your legal responsibilities. Committees are also good for team-building as they allow less confident governors to find a role. Even with committees I think most governors find two meetings essential. Some have one 'legal' meeting and one to look at important school issues in a less formal setting, with perhaps some appropriate key staff present. You may find that some keen governors will jump at the idea (the ones you meet in the holidays!) and that a few don't want further commitments. This is a good test, and I am all for pushing for high standards and seeing the passengers drop off.

Secret ballots

 Can we elect our chair by secret ballot?

The only regular agenda item which governors are legally *obliged* to decide by secret vote is the ballot on grant-maintained status. Otherwise governors themselves normally decide how to conduct their business, though some LEAs through their instruments of government have made electing chair by secret ballot a standard practice in their area. I take it yours is not one, but if a majority on your governing body think a secret vote would help you, you can still decide to elect your chair that way.

In the past my instinct was not to like secret procedures and to be sorry if groups found them necessary. I now think, however, that if governors do not feel able to elect the chair they want –

and this is often so – a secret vote may be the answer. For many years election of parent governors at a meeting by show of hands was very common, and it was found to favour the socially confident both as candidates and voters. The government therefore provided by law for secret ballots both for parent and teacher governors. Within governing bodies the issue is also in part of confidence and maturity. The government made the new rule on grant-maintained voting because they feared intimidation by powerful people with strong views. Intimidation takes many forms, however, and if people for any reason do not feel free to express their true opinions they must be helped. Being too nice is also often a problem. If this is your problem I recommend you to shut your eyes and think hard about the children. Better to offend an adult than damage a child.

Resignation of the chair in mid-term

 Our chairman is being sent abroad by his firm at Easter and will be away for a year or more. There is so much work for governors that he has said he is willing to resign and hand over to the vice-chair. Most of us have been very disappointed in her as she has been a poor attender and not very interested. Must we agree?

 If your chairman does not resign the vice-chair will act on his behalf until the end of his year of office, when there will be a new election. If he does resign there is legally no automatic succession of the vice-chair: you would then have to elect a new chair straight away, and would have a free choice.

Do we have to have so many papers tabled at the meeting?

 At almost every meeting we get long papers circulated which we have to try to discuss. The chairman gives us reading time, but when they are complicated I do not always feel competent to contribute after such a hasty perusal.

 This is a bad habit and all too easy to get into. In a few cases it can't be helped: a late circular, a budget print-out which only comes at certain fixed times, an urgent matter which has blown up. But far too many papers are tabled which could well have been done in time for circulation if the initiator had thought about it.

First, we should not be using our precious meeting time doing something which we could have done at home, namely reading. Have you ever heard teachers criticized for regularly using up lessons on 'silent reading'? Second, the whole point is to think about things as well as read them, and it is bound to diminish the quality of discussion if papers have been only hastily skimmed. Finally, and most important of all, it is an instrument of inequality. People read at different rates, have varying levels of education and knowledge of the issues and the jargon, and English may be a second language for some. You can't eliminate these differences, but if you give people the chance to read at their own pace and in privacy, look things up, ask questions, it does reduce them to a minimum. In short, carry on complaining.

Visitors to meetings

 A teacher in our primary school has just completed a curriculum development of great originality and shown a lot of initiative. I suggested we should invite her to our next meeting to talk to the governors about it. The head said certainly not: it is for him to decide, he said, what visitors come to meetings, and all curriculum matters should be reported to the governors through the head. What is your view?

 I sometimes despair of everybody ever working from the same rulebook. It is not for the head teacher to decide about visitors: the law clearly states that the governing body decides what if any visitors should attend meetings. Your suggestion accords with the best practice and thousands of governing bodies will this week be asking teachers to come – often all teachers in rotation – to talk to governors about aspects of curriculum, the more so if they have done something special. Your head seems to feel threatened by different perspectives, especially those arising from great talent: perhaps you would do better to suggest that *he* chooses a different staff member each time to come and talk to governors so that you get better informed about the school and staff get to know governors. He may be happy if the situation is more controlled. But someone should tell him that governors decide on their policy about visitors.

Do we really have to make all decisions at meetings?

 As chair of governors I am concerned about the need to have so many decisions made at a meeting of the whole governing body. Do not misunderstand - I think it is wholly right that power should stay there. But the practicalities defeat me. Finance issues are efficiently covered by a monthly committee, premises cared for by another, pupil and teacher discipline cases if they arise by an elected group of three, and so on. But how can I possibly summon sixteen busy people on all the occasions when no delegation is allowed or when a matter has to be remitted to an elected group at short notice? So often too we are locked into LEA processes where the timing is critical or at the mercy of DFE random missiles. Last term we appointed a new deputy head – special meeting to endorse the choice. A late national curriculum circular totally threw our options when the governors had only just met. A girl was permanently excluded and because the head had enlisted the advice of the exclusion panel informally beforehand and they had been much involved in the matter I felt we needed a fresh group to hear the parents. I confess I rang around for approval to my choice. I confess, too, that the annual report to parents was circulated in draft by post to the governors for final approval, after many had contributed. How serious are these technical breaches? Surely it is not always necessary to meet?

 Most governing bodies would envy yours their well-informed and conscientious chair. Many break the rules you refer to. Strictly speaking decisions which have to be made by the whole governing body can only legally be made at a meeting. Of course you will delegate as much as you think wise to committees on subjects where delegation is possible, e.g. finance, care of premises. For the rest it *is* important that matters are discussed and that individuals can hear all the arguments. A governing body is more than the sum of its parts. But some breaches are a lot worse than others. I would think there are many governing bodies which circulate the annual report by post, and as long as there is plenty of time to comment and as long as there has been wide participation in planning its content and contributing to it, I would not think this was too sinful. It is much more serious if the governors do not meet to ratify a senior staff appointment, or if the group which hears representations from parents on exclusion or a staff appeal, or selects a senior member of staff has not been elected by the whole governing body at a meeting. Decisions hurting individuals are the most likely to be challenged and can be overturned on procedural grounds even if the merits are not in dispute.

Here are some practical tips. First, encourage your head to start every meeting with a preview of matters which have to be decided in the *next* three months as well as a review of events past. Make sure it includes things like deadlines for admission policy decisions and other LEA fixed points like minor works programme planning, as well as school matters like posts to be filled, and dates for options and other information to parents to go out. Then you can plan. Second, ensure that your governors have made enough contingency decisions to cover most likely needs. For instance elect a second panel for pupil and staff disciplinary decisions so that there are always fresh governors who have been properly elected to hear appeals if the first has been 'contaminated' by too much involvement: elect a reserve while you are at it.

Third, remember that governors can in some cases decide on a *system* for doing something as well as the action in detail, e.g. governors to be asked to help with teacher appointments in alphabetical order or in accordance with their special subject attachment. Even in a really tricky case governors can decide on a formula which gives the chair several options based on a series of variables you don't know at the time.

Finally, be satisfied that you are obviously a thorough and thoughtful chair with a strong feeling about doing things democratically, and your best will probably be pretty good compared with most that goes on.

Can we make decisions by post or phone?

When a matter legally requires the decision of the whole governing body, does it have to be at a meeting or is a postal or telephone consultation adequate? Second, can a committee (without delegated powers) make a decision if there happens to be a quorum of the full governing body present?

Strictly speaking a meeting is the proper place to make any decision requiring the whole governing body. After all it is not the same if governors can't hear the reactions of colleagues and make up their minds in the light of debate and in a considered way, without pressure. I suspect many governing bodies approve final drafts circulated by post from time to time (e.g., of annual reports to parents which strictly require a full governing body decision) and if governors have agreed to the procedure, if there has been full discussion of the content at an earlier stage and if any significant changes suggested by individuals are the subject of further consultation, I doubt if the matter would be challenged, though technically irregular. But you would not agree to appoint a new head that way or go to parental ballot on grant-maintained status!

On your second question, a legal decision can be taken at what was originally planned as a committee meeting provided that all governors are informed in advance (seven days unless the chair decides that it is urgent) that it is to be regarded as a special governors' meeting and provided that it is quorate for the matter to be decided. It is not enough that there 'happen' to be enough people there for a quorum if it has not been billed as a full meeting. It may often be convenient to give notice to convert a committee meeting to a governors' meeting in this way if, for instance, the budget needs to be approved or some matter has come up unexpectedly, since a number of governors will already have saved the date and in a well-run governing body all governors will know the date and the subject-matter of the meeting anyway. But it would be sensible for the clerk to check that enough governors can come to make it quorate to avoid wasting members' time.

A timetabled agenda?

 Do you agree with an agenda where every item is timed? Ours comes in that form – this is the chairman's wish and I accept he is a busy man – but I do not think one hour every term is really enough to make all the necessary decisions for a big comprehensive. Some items have only two minutes' allowance which allows no discussion at all, and the only ones which have ten or fifteen minutes are less important things like the catering arrangements for the sixth form end-of-year party.

 Your complaint is not really so much about a time-tabled agenda as a one-hour meeting. I think it is absurd, and the only conclusion one can come to is that the governing body is not operating at all, that the chair has everything sewn up, and that the agenda is a means of control not a programme for a meeting. You must tackle these more fundamental problems first, I am afraid. If others are dissatisfied also you must plan an effective protest, and when the time comes elect a chair who does have time for a proper meeting and who does want other governors to play a part. Remember your chair is there with your consent.

A good chair who is also a team builder may well decide to have a rough plan for the meeting, with a suggested target finishing time, so that governors can discuss properly the really meaty items and therefore voluntarily restrain themselves from rambling on about things which are interesting but not so important. This plan for the use of the time should only be a suggestion, however, and opportunity should always be given for governors to accept or modify it. We all have different views of what is important and we operate by mutual agreement. Remember it is your meeting, your agenda and - yes - your chair.

Rescinding an earlier decision

 At our last meeting but one we made a decision on a very difficult issue. The governors were divided but in the end after a quite emotional argument we voted and there was a clear majority. The last meeting was a special meeting called solely – we thought – to approve a change in the budget. There was a reference on the agenda to the controversial matter in question, but so phrased as to suggest it was just to report developments. Attendance was not as good as

usual because of the shorter notice, and the argument was re-opened and this time the decision was reversed. At least four governors who had voted the other way were not there. We felt this was sharp practice, taking advantage of the absence of certain governors to get a decision overturned. What do you think?

Strangely this subject has never come up in my postbag before, and in a month it has come up twice. Regulation 20 of the governors' regulations (SI 1503 of 1989) provides that in an aided or special agreement school a previous decision can only be rescinded if the agenda for the second meeting makes it clear that this is being proposed. An amendment in 1991 extended this to all schools. The intention is clearly to prevent the kind of manipulation you suggest occurred in your case, and also to give governors a chance to think about such a serious matter in advance. So the reversal of your original decision does not appear to be legal.

Right to get an item on the agenda

You are always saying governors should be aware how to get things on the agenda. I know what the process is, but what can I do if the chair and head, who with the clerk meet to agree the agenda, persistently refuse to accept what to me is an important item because it does not suit their angle to have it discussed? They seem to have the power to suppress anything they do not like, so the idea of the governing body having any control over the business of the meeting is a fraud.

You have made a good point, which I have thought about a great deal too. The agenda *is* the responsibility of the whole governing body and, technically, when you suffer the kind of frustration you describe, you can bring it up at the next meeting and ask for a vote on whether the item should be added to this agenda or placed on the next. But there are several snags. First of all maybe it can't wait till the next meeting. Second, if you succeed in getting it included in the current agenda nobody will have had a chance to prepare for it, so you can't have a proper discussion. Finally, sometimes on a governing body there will be just one person who is prepared to 'stand up to authority' so no support is forthcoming.

I believe the solution would be a new rule that any three

governors requesting an item on the agenda had a right to its inclusion, just as three can call a special meeting. This would not, of course, mean that one or two governors could not ask for an item, merely that three secured automatic inclusion. I must add that there is a well-informed school of thought of the opinion that this right already exists. I hope they are correct, but I do not know 'where it says' and meanwhile the frustration you describe is the reality for many governors.

When you talk at the beginning of a year, as I hope you do, about organizing your work, agreeing procedures etc., there is no reason why your governing body should not adopt such a rule for itself if you can persuade colleagues. Alternatively you could try to get the support of a few colleagues when you ask for an item: it would be harder to refuse.

No prizes for being right

 I raised at our last meeting a query on a school policy which I was not happy about. I had told the head and chair in advance that I was going to raise it and it came up naturally under the head's report. There was some blustering and resistance to my point, but I got a great deal of support too. Indeed the practice I had questioned was quietly dropped only a few weeks after the meeting. I was amazed when we got the minutes with our next agenda to find the matter was not even referred to, and I got nowhere trying to get it included.

 There are a number of points here. First of all, if governors have a discussion which does not actually conclude with a clear agreed recommendation on the action to be taken – even if it is that no action be taken! – they are not being very effective. They also lose the chance to insist that the discussion be recorded, since minutes are not normally a blow-by-blow account of everything that was said. Thus anyone who has a reason for excluding an item or asking for it to be excluded has the excuse that it did not lead anywhere. What is more, if governors want to be sure something is recorded, they should ask for it at the time, and if colleagues agree they can even settle the form of words on the spot. If they do not agree I am afraid you have lost that one.

The second point concerns when and to whom draft minutes are circulated. It is good practice to circulate them as soon as possible after the meeting and give every governor a chance to comment on matters of accuracy within, say, a week. This is because draft minutes become public documents as soon as the chair has approved them, and it does not make sense if anyone can come in from the street and see a document before those who were present have set eyes on it. At the next meeting when the minutes are formally ratified, additions can still be made, but even then a majority must accept them.

So much for the formalities. Now to the questions behind the question. I think what you are saying is not so much that you want the record complete but that, since your criticism seems to have been accepted, you want credit where credit is due and those concerned to have the decency to accept they were wrong. This is natural. But you have the satisfaction of having raised an issue which led to something good happening for the pupils, and because pride plays a part in all relationships this might not happen if you insisted on the severed head on a plate as well. In other words it is sometimes a choice between the name and the game.

Role of non-governors attending meetings

   What role have non-governor teachers in governors' meetings? Our head attends, though he is not a governor. So do the deputies. The latter play a vigorous part, expressing strong views and sometimes even trying to cast a vote. They also serve on committees. We do not dispute their right to be present but have they any right to behave like de facto *governors?*

   To deal first with the head, although you have not said he is a problem. Unlike the deputies, he is there by legal right, and if he has chosen not to be a governor his role is that of professional adviser. He will naturally give the governors his views on where the interests of the school lie in any particular matter, as well as offering information and guidance on any issue where his position as head of the school gives him relevant insights. He has no vote.

As for the deputies, in strictly legal terms they are there because the governors have invited them, though in practice this may have amounted to acquiescing passively in their presence. If you did not any longer want them there, you could exclude them. I would not recommend this. First, because it is heavy-handed and confrontational and, second, because I actually think it is good practice to invite deputies (at the very least in turn) to governors' meetings. It is important in-service training apart from the contribution they make. Many schools involve a deputy instead of the head in the main committees to which their role is relevant, but as I expect you know they can't chair these.

It is quite acceptable for visitors to governors' meetings to speak. There will be information they can offer, and I would not even rule out setting out the pros and cons of an issue on which they have a great deal of knowledge as long as it is done with scrupulous objectivity. Since they do not have a vote, however, any expression of opinion is a very sensitive matter since it could influence those who do have votes, and on matters where there is clearly more than one possible view I would not think it acceptable for a visitor to express support for any of them.

It is really the job of the chair to see that governors' meetings are properly conducted, though it is always harder when breaches of rules or conventions have already taken place unchallenged. I would think in your case the chair should speak frankly to the head about it and ask him to make it clear to the deputies that they are there as observers by invitation and that they should maintain a rather lower profile to avoid putting their attendance in jeopardy.

Do grant-maintained schools have to have a clerk?

 Ours is a grant-maintained school which acquired grant-maintained status over two years ago. We have not yet appointed a clerk. Is this legal?

 I think you will find that your instrument of government (made in the case of a grant-maintained school by the Secretary of State) says that there 'shall' be a clerk. In the instrument I have seen it is paragraph 10(1). No time limit is mentioned but I think non-appointment in over two years would be considered irregular.

Role and remuneration of LEA clerks

 Our LEA expect officers to offer their services as clerks to governing bodies – though of course governors are free to make other arrangements if they want to. We get no overtime payments, just time off in lieu, and this is largely evening work. We have no opportunity to refuse. Could you comment on this and also say what the duties of a clerk are?

 I assume that when the LEA used to clerk governing bodies automatically the same arrangements applied. If so I cannot see that you have any new cause for complaint. If the conditions have been changed I hope that they have been agreed with your union or professional association representatives, and if not you should discuss the matter with them, though I think time off in lieu is quite common.

What is new is that the governors now 'employ' the clerk in the sense that they have an allowance to spend on it and some choice how to arrange clerking, e.g. whether to ask for your services or make arrangements themselves. Thus the question of the clerk's responsibilities are for negotiation between that person and the governors, ranging from simply taking minutes to assuming much more responsibility for the proper conduct of governors' business and advising them on their powers and duties. It should be clear between you from the outset what is expected.

Teachers on pay committees

 What do you think about teacher governors being on pay committees? This must be a question which is now coming up often. Neither our head nor our chairperson favours it, and the head says it is against the advice of his professional association. I sometimes wonder what is the point of being a teacher governor when we don't have a say in anything important or controversial.

 I realize that I am taking on some heavy-weight opponents, in that at least two professional associations and more than one LEA has already said that it is better for teacher governors not to be on pay committees. However, I feel as certain as I can be that the words 'an interest more than the generality of teachers', which occur in the regulations to clarify the restriction on teacher governors taking part in decisions from which they stand to gain, make it unlawful for anyone to prohibit it in this case. It is of course a different matter if the teacher does not want to be involved: any of us has the right to say no. The DFE has taken such trouble in successive versions of the regulations to avoid any but essential restrictions on the right to participate, that I am sure the intention of the words quoted was to enable teacher governors to take part in decisions which concern all staff but do not concern the governor individually and uniquely.

I will stick my neck out still further and say that I think it is good practice for the school to have teacher governors participate. It prevents any suspicion that decisions are being made in a secret and arbitrary way, which is destructive even if unfounded, and it gives other staff confidence if their representative is there. If anything comes up on a pay committee of special application to that individual teacher, he/she must of course withdraw.

8 Working together as a team

A team is a group of people with a common purpose. They strive for excellence in individual performance but not, of course, at the expense of others, since a team weaves its members' complementary skills into a seamless whole to serve its ends. Members of a good team look after and protect each other and are loyal to each other. They share the work. They are eager to learn and develop. They know and abide by the rules which safeguard every individual's space. They accept responsibility for the quality of their work together.

In this chapter you will find many examples of teams which are not working: A and B teams, 'kitchen cabinets', small groups or individuals who seem to have hi-jacked the power and influence.

Nowhere in educational law will you find anything about the duties and powers of a school governor. That is because individual governors have no power whatsoever. It is only the governing body, working together and making decisions together, which has any power to act, advise, warn, sometimes even change things. Many governors forget that, and then the trouble starts. Whenever schools get into a mess it is usually because individuals have tried to solve things by themselves, or the governing body has been careless with its precious responsibility and allowed it to slide around. The outcome is nearly always disaster. That is why in so many answers I stress the importance of loyalty to the group and its corporate decisions.

Scattered through the book you will find references to many aspects of team work, and now is the time to bring them all together and look at the elements of success. Especially relevant are Chapters 6 and 7, particularly the introduction to the latter which deals with the working-together rules which, if understood and observed, protect the governing body against fragmentation of its responsibility. The way in which meetings are conducted can also exclude or include people, welcome or discourage participation, assume agreement instead of encouraging people to contribute. Chapter 6 is important because it stresses the need to allow individuals to communicate with and speak for those they represent, and if this need is frustrated some members are marginalized before you begin. There will always be powerful individuals in any group, and it is important to enlist the strength of the group to protect its weaker members. Every governor who remains silent in the face of power games is guilty. If bad things happen it is because we all let them happen. We are too slow finding our glasses, too prone to say 'I know that was not right but I did not know where it said '– or simply too nice.

A good team has a common purpose. Governors should find time to share their common purpose often, because it is the cement that binds them together. An ex-Prime Minister said: 'If we don't have a star to guide us by, we shall be prisoners of our agenda.' We do not stop often enough to put into words what is special to us about our school, that magic that keeps us at it despite weariness and frustration.

Members of a good team are willing to learn. Do not forget about introducing a system for every governor to spend some time in the school on a regular basis, observing children at work. Encourage each other to go to training sessions. Go together. Put training on the agenda.

Good team members know and observe the rules. I have talked about that. They look after each other and especially their not so forceful members, the shy, the new, those who feel they have not had much education, those whose first language is not English, those who are having difficulty representing others. They look after teachers when someone tries to restrict unreasonably their right to participate in governors' duties. They look after parent governors if somebody tries to say it is not their job to listen to parents' concerns.

A successful team shares the work. Are A and B teams visible in your committee structure? Make sure all interest groups are evenly spread over your committees, and have some system for sharing the paper work as well.

Finally, a good team accepts and shares responsibility for its own work, never blaming 'somebody' for things they failed to do themselves. That means planning, vigilance and care for colleagues.

Checklist: are you a good team?

O Do you know about the skills and experience of your colleagues?

O Do they know about yours?

O Can you have a healthy disagreement and keep your shared aims?

O Do you talk often about what you value in the school and your aims for it?

O Do you spend enough time establishing principles and good practices, rather than meeting every issue head-on?

O Do you feel that every governor contributes?

O Are you satisfied that there are no governors with private agendas

O Does everyone leave the meeting feeling they have had a say?

O Do you have good systems of work-sharing involving everybody?

O Are all interest groups fairly represented on committees?

O Do parent governors and teacher governors play a full part?

O Do your teacher governors contribute confidently and without fear?

O Would someone always intervene to protect a governor who was for any reason being prevented from making a full contibution

O Do you have a system for every governor to commit some regular time to involvement in the school? Or do you feel there are some who won't?

O Do you spend enough time organizing your work properly?

O Do you feel that you have a free choice of chair?

O Does your chair see his/her main role as team-building?

O Are you always clear about what you have decided?

O Do you spend time looking *forward*? Or are you agenda-driven?

O Do you realize that looking ahead is the only way to make sure you are involved at the proper time, and not too late?

O Are you all loyal to majority decisions?

A governing body in conflict

 Our governing body is deeply divided. A certain faction is hostile to our hard-working and enthusiastic head (who is too 'modern' for them), even to the point of saying openly that they want to get him dismissed. This campaign dominates everything they do and important tasks get sidelined. The parent governors (of whom I am one), like nearly all parents, are really supportive of the school and so are all but one of the four LEA governors. The troublesome group consists of three of the co-opted governors and the remaining LEA governor. How can we deal with this?

 A bit of rapid arithmetic suggests that, as so often, eleven people are allowing themselves to be terrorized by four. I have not counted the head since presumably this campaign against him is only pursued indirectly if at all in his presence, so that he is unable to fight his corner. If the majority are united they should be able to deal with it.

I assume that the dissident group are some sort of educational fundamentalists wanting the school to go back to basics. If it is a successful school you must make sure you have the ammunition on this and encourage your head to use it at meetings. Speak up strongly yourselves too. Try and have the debate about teaching styles and methods, if that is what it is, in the open at meetings, by having teachers in turn to talk about their work, rather than letting it simmer under the surface in the form of a personal vendetta against the head. In all your personal contacts with this group (and for obvious reasons much of what you need to say can't be said at meetings, hence their success in dividing the governing body), do point out that this school like others has to follow the national curriculum and hasn't the freedom to freak out that they imagine; that the parents are largely supportive; that you can't dismiss a head for being 'modern'; and that it is highly dangerous - and could at a later stage be very expensive - to talk about such things in anything but a structured way and within very firm rules. Point out that theirs is a minority view and that governors have to be united to do anything really difficult.

Are you satisfied that enough is done in your school to demonstrate directly the success of the methods used by opening up the process to governors and parents? Have you a system for *all* governors to spend time in school, with no exceptions tolerated? Such observation is worth ten times its weight in argument, especially with teachers briefed to make the connections between the methods and the goals. I say this because it is very hard to fight prejudice if its victims are unwilling to demonstrate the success of their policies. As an outsider I learned a long time ago – rather to my surprise – that there were just as many advocates of child-centred learning who were authoritarian as there were more old-fashioned operators, and they don't do their cause any favours. They even sometimes suffer grievously for their unwillingness to debate their convictions. In your case it may be that this sort of defensiveness is driving the argument underground and personalizing it. I don't need to tell you that it is also making your governing body very unproductive and probably, by polarizing attitudes, preventing all of you from being the critical friends a school needs. Perhaps someone the head listens to can convince him that there has to be more open debate about school policies for his own protection.

Governors who challenge the school's educational ethos

 As a head I want to work co-operatively with my governors, but what can you do about a vocal group such as I have among mine whose idea of 'a good school' is at odds with our beliefs and policies as a staff and who wage constant battle against those policies? They have a leader, of course, a powerful political appointee, who overawes everybody else (what the majority think I do not know), but he is supported by a couple of pushy parent governors and one co-optee from business. We know where we are going as a school and I do not relish spending so much energy on self-styled well-wishers who are on a different wavelength.

 I expect your dissident governors would think your letter arrogant, but I know from the rest of it that you are defending something you deeply believe in.

But that is beside the point. You unintentionally provide a very good argument for all those who have tried to turn education upside down from 1988 onwards, by showing the strength of the tendency to define 'a good school' as that which most of your generation of professionals would accept, regardless of strong feelings by some very powerful people. Those feelings are there outside your gates, in the press, on the buses, among a significant number of parents, and they are almost regarded as self-evident by many. Outside the school you can scarcely hope any more to argue your case, but the governing body gives every school a chance to engage with a range of opinions within a very controlled and favourable structure if it can only use the opportunity. Continuous re-statement of your own strongly-held convictions (whether they are on the broad curriculum, child-centred focus, more varied indices of success, special needs, ability groupings, behaviour policy) will only strengthen the suspicion that your minds are closed to other influences. You stand a chance if you are open with all governors, encourage them to come closer and observe your ideas working for themselves, listen to other views with respect, and above all do your team-building with governors in a way which will empower those who might support you if they were liberated to do so.

You may have a bad case of A and B teams, with one powerful A team leader, and I almost feel embarrassed about saying so often that there is no way of curbing abuse of power except by empowering others. From the size of your school I would say you have sixteen governors. Among those who do not publicly rubbish your policies you must have some who would sing your tune if you provided them with enough silence to do so, and the confidence to speak from the strength of their own observation. In time they may even elect different leaders.

But these potential allies need your help. If you look carefully at how your people-power is spread over tasks, and how much pressure there is on all to see the school at work, you may find some clues. You also need to consider how you handle diffident governors or respond to non-conforming but strong, legitimate and sincerely held opinions about what schools are for. My final comment may be totally unjustified but I have looked at your catchment area, and I wonder whether the school registers high expectations of pupils from all classes? Making too many allowances for home background, though well-meant, is the source of much of the criticism levelled in recent years against 'progressive' education.

Another governor tries to go it alone

 How as a head can I deal with a new governor who is making waves in the school by interfering in the detail of classroom practice and school organization? I am willing to involve governors in discussions of the budget, the curriculum, and policies of all kinds but they respond very little. I can't cope with interference by individuals in how the school is run. It is not for myself but my staff that I am concerned.

 I know that this is difficult to cope with. In my experience such governors rarely have disruptive intentions and they often feel very positive about the school when you pin them down. Mostly the trouble with an inexperienced governor is role confusion combined with a desire to be active in some way. Often the really supportive PTA parent who has always been a tower of strength thinks being a governor means 'going in to make sure everything is all right', even looking for some trivial point to raise.

Training and induction processes should encompass clear guidance about roles, and it is a pity that this can't be available *before* problems can arise, so that keen but misguided governors don't start on the wrong foot and have to get told off. A sympathetic chair could easily give a new governor a bit of counselling before the first meeting and explain that individually we have no power; that although we have a major job to do it is as members of a team; that we go into school to learn; and that our involvement is at policy level and certainly not to question the way teachers do their day-by-day work.

Then it is up to you as a head to find some real work for these idle hands to do. Many governors meddle because they don't have any genuine opportunity to involve themselves at strategic level, so don't feel ownership of the framework within which teachers operate, and it all seems a game of pretend. It is always a good idea to review our practices from time to time and ensure that governors are brought in at a level on which they can contribute – which is often more the brain-storming stage than the endorsement of beautifully argued documents. Many heads whose desire to involve governors in policy is genuine do need to think more about how to do it. However open they are with information and however willing to accept suggestions, they do not offer governors anything to get hold of. They may mistake lack of response for indifference when it is really bewilderment on governors' part about how they can contribute. This is probably the most difficult problem we confront at the present stage of our development.

Governors who do not contribute much

 What can we do about governor colleagues who contribute little or nothing? Most of us work hard but there are always some passengers and apart from needing every governor's contribution, it has a bad effect on our morale.

 I hope when the present generation of governors has worked its term there will be a number who will realize they have not pulled their weight and will go. If the governing body has established a 'culture' of commitment and comparable effort made by all (I say comparable rather than equal because individuals do make different contributions), it will be an effective source of pressure. Otherwise I have two favourite answers. One is that governors should always find time at the beginning of a year to plan the work. The second is that this message is followed through by establishing precise and rigorous routines for every governor to get involved, not just in committees and working groups, but in some regular contact with and responsibility in the school. Whether it is governor of the month, governor of the subject, or governor attached to a class, it must be clear that no exemptions are intended. And there must be a slot at meetings for individuals to report on what they have done. As with weight watchers' clubs, it is not the diet they hand out which does the trick but the public weighing. In other words, shame.

First footings

You often say how important the first meeting of the school year is to the working together process. Could you elaborate?

One or two obvious reasons first. It is the meeting at which you elect your chair, a vital decision which many governing bodies seem unable to make freely. You are more likely to have new colleagues and new school staff. You have all had a long period away from the school and a chance to reflect on how your governing body is working or not working.

Most of all, however, this is an occasion when you can most easily stand back as a group to look at how you organize yourselves, to plan your work and to solve long-standing problems. You can't just pipe up on any Monday afternoon in February: 'This governing body is getting far too cliquey,'; 'Who elected that idiot to the chair?'; 'We aren't all pulling our weight,'; or 'We're just rubber-stamps.' These common complaints have acquired too many human faces for that and you need to distance the problem from the feelings of those who contribute to it or suffer from it.

Nobody will turn a hair if you suggest that at the first meeting it is a good idea to have a permanent agenda item 'Organizing our work'. I will come on to the contents of this item in a minute, but first consider having a brief discussion about the role of the chair, the qualities of a good chair, and the kind of relationship you want with yours. If you seriously plan a change, you must of course have got your act together and have alternatives ready. Either way it provides a non-hurtful means of establishing a few markers.

Now to planning the work. If it is not standard practice, I would put top of the list that every meeting should include –perhaps as part of the head's report – a brief indication of the matters which will require decisions in the *next* three months, as well as a review of the last. This is the only way to turn the governing body round 180 degrees to face the future, and ensure that we are not rubber stamps. Meetings and activity should then be adjusted to ensure that we put that building job to the Council's minor works committee, fix the budget, agree the options before the parents' letter is due out, respond to the circular, work on the prospectus and properly plan our own report to parents.

Second, we want to review our committees and their terms of reference and membership. This is the time to put right any A and B team tendencies and ensure that governors of all interest groups – and new governors – are spread over all the tasks. We must be crystal clear about what we are delegating if we are to keep hold of our responsibility. We also need to see if we can share out the paper work in any helpful way (getting individual governors to prepare and present issues, for instance) and talk about paper distribution generally. Do we want to see *all* correspondence (careful, now!) and if not would we like a list each time of documents received and have them kept in a box accessible to all?

Third, we need to establish some system for *all* governors to see the school at work. Only this way can we make good decisions and be good ambassadors. This should be an expression of our high expectations of each other and our no-slacking culture. It can be a duty governor of the month, whereby each governor is the first point of contact for the school for a whole month (fixed a year ahead) to plant the tree, attend the parents' meeting, help select a teacher, give out swimming badges, whatever arises, and also undertakes to spend at least half a day observing some manageable aspect of pupils' learning. An alternative is to link a governor to a subject area or (especially in primary schools) a class, going up with that class and getting to know the children well. All activity must be reported to full governors (public shame does work). This discussion should always end in a review of what the governors see as appropriate behaviour when visiting, including the obvious courtesies, and high-lighting that individuals have no power and go in only to learn.

Any bad habits which have grown up can be tackled impersonally at this meeting too. You will have your own list, which may include tabling papers when they could just as easily have gone with the agenda, undermining majority decisions, private meetings of two or more governors which are not reported to others, or gossiping about matters concerning individuals which have come to governors. This is also the time to establish your information needs and have early warning of school events you would wish to attend.

When feelings must be kept to yourself

 I think my governing body have made a very unfair decision on a redundancy issue. I had my dissent recorded but I was outvoted. I have told the young teacher concerned who lives in our village that I was opposed to her being made redundant and I have also raised it on the parish council which I represent. This has led to my being ostracized by fellow governors. Am I not entitled to my opinion?

 Yes, and you went as far as was proper in recording your dissent, especially as it would have certainly been a confidential item which you should not in any circumstances discuss outside the school. Apart from the confidentiality, however, it is totally unacceptable to dissociate yourself publicly from a majority decision properly made. We should all be loyal to our colleagues in public however strongly we feel. You should either apologize, pleading inexperience or, if you cannot accept the decision at all, resign.

Should a head be loyal to governors' decisions?

 Are head teachers who have opted to be governors bound by the governing body's decisions when they have been outvoted? Are they at liberty to take or advocate another course of action within the school, in talking to the LEA or parents, or to indicate that they disapprove of the majority decision?

 I reply without knowledge of the matter at issue, of course, but in general every governor must be loyal to majority decisions and the head in this respect should abide by the same rules. Every head has the choice to be a governor or not: 'opting in' has its advantages, as most heads seem to believe, but it carries responsibilities and constraints as well. In the cases where a governor feels so strongly that he/she wants dissent recorded in the minutes – and this should not be overused – there will be the satisfaction that the dissent is public knowledge. Even then it would be very wrong for that governor to speak or act against the majority wishes or try to persuade others that a different course should be adopted.

The majority are not always right

 You always emphasize how important it is for governors to be loyal to corporate decisions and, of course, in general I agree. But sometimes the minority are right, not just in their own eyes but factually, legally, in terms of generally accepted good practice, by a variety of quite provable standards. Often the majority have not given a thought to what they are doing until the moment they shipwreck your reasoned argument or passionate conviction, have little knowledge or commitment. It is very hard to suffer defeat in these circumstances and stay quiet.

 I know. Many will echo your sentiments. In a system which is new, evolving and unequally resourced with information and support, I know well that the governors who are going it alone are just as likely to be the saints and martyrs as the dangerous oddballs.

In a sense, however, this is true of much decision making which goes by the name of democracy, and in the long run is not it safer and healthier if people have to work and wait for the acceptance of their 'reasoned argument or passionate conviction'? Large numbers affected by the outcome may be closer to the majority: their acceptance is necessary and can't always be hurried. People with a light in their eyes are the ones who achieve things, but they can be dangerous as well and the majority have a healthy mistrust of them and take a lot of convincing. You always have another chance to step up the persuasion, and if the obstacle is inertia or ignorance, and not genuine disagreement, it will yield in time.

I do not mean to be negative and there are hopeful factors at work. First, training of governors is getting better all the time, and if we can work for a culture in which governors who are unwilling to learn are not easily excused, we shall soon at least reduce the number of bad decisions based on wrong information and unfamiliarity with good practice. Second, if we were more insistent that LEAs don't duck their responsibility for intervening when governors are getting onto a seriously wrong track or where relationships are bad we could rescue a lot of martyrs. Good heads can do a great deal in this direction too. Third, governors are slowly learning to make time now and then – without the pressure of contentious issues – to talk about their own development and working rules.

A kitchen cabinet?

 Our head teacher says he is keen to work in partnership with governors, and in that we are lucky. He is also anxious not to have his hands tied in managing the school smoothly on a day-by-day basis, and aware that we meet infrequently and meanwhile have our livings to earn. He is determined to run an efficient 'business', and one of his suggestions is that we establish a very small policy group consisting of the chair (who has taken early retirement and can spare time, and who is by the way an LEA appointee), the vice-chair who is a business governor and more or less his own boss, and another co-opted governor from a local college with whom the head gets on well. The idea is that if decisions have to be made on advertising a post, authorizing expenditure for some unforeseen purpose, confirming the permanent exclusion of a pupil, starting disciplinary proceedings, should it ever arise, against a staff member, or changing the options, he has a group of experienced people whom he can contact quickly for endorsement of the action. What is your view?

 I don't like it, in a nutshell. Democracy can be slow and the reasons behind this suggestion are understandable. The framework of school government does not, however, lend itself to a 'kitchen cabinet', and what the head proposes is really removing control from the governing body. It is highly undesirable for one group of people to be carrying out all those functions, especially as they do not include any parent or teacher governor and apparently have either been self-selected or chosen by the head.

First of all there are more functions governors cannot delegate than functions they are legally able to (see your DFE *Guide to the Law* for a list: changes in the options for instance is certainly not a decision for a small group). A considerable number of vital responsibilities require decision by the governing body at a meeting. But even if a single small group were freely *elected* by the governing body, and only given such powers as can legally be delegated, I should still consider it far too big a range of functions to be in so few hands.

The great virtue of committees indeed is that apart from being efficient they give more people a chance to participate at a more detailed level and in a small and less formal group in the work of the school. A governing body which takes seriously its corporate responsibility (and therefore the conscious consent of each of its members to what is done in their name), will spread the delegated duties as even-handedly as possible over all interest groups, and work hard to achieve something like equivalent contribution from each member. It is only right then that such committees should meet reasonably often as a group and communicate well with head, relevant staff and governors about what they are doing.

Much can be done to solve the problems your head has identified. Committees elected by the governors with well-defined functions, meeting regularly and communicating well, go some way. Good planning of full meetings so that all necessary decisions and guidance are given and clearly expressed, continue the process. Discretion wherever possible within defined limits for the head (e.g. in virement between budget headings up to a certain level, in advertising posts within agreed staffing structures at the appropriate grading, in progressing maintenance work when the scheme and the funding have been broadly agreed) all smooth the path, and we should all be considerate about the daily pressures of running a school and make it as straightforward as we can. Above all, however, the governors should have drawn up clear policies on matters within their competence *before* specific issues come up so that the head and staff have proper guidelines. Half the battle in achieving efficiency without sacrifice of democracy is for all concerned – head as well – to look ahead at matters where decisions may be required before they meet again, rather than allowing themselves to be totally agenda-driven. The head can greatly help governors to identify these areas, and his reports to them at full meetings should always look forwards as well as backwards.

Please think hard about what you are proposing. Whenever governors get into a mess I find the cause is quite likely to be failure of all governors to be responsible and vigilant, and allowing power to slide into too few hands.

A bad case of A and B teams

Our governing body has a policy and resources committee (just like the Council!) and all the powerful governors are on it – the LEA group, a couple of co-optees from business, the head. The rest of us, including mere parent and teacher governors, are on committees dealing with pupil welfare, buildings maintenance, community links. Finance, admissions, curriculum and staffing policy are all dealt with in the first committee and do not come to governors. Meetings are short because reports from the other committees are dismissed in moments. Help!

This is a classic case of the A and the B team. I know it is not uncommon and I know it is difficult when groups of people assume power as a right, but I can only say again that we must grow up and assume our responsibilities. If you have five LEA governors, for instance, you will have five parents, two teachers and four co-opted governors other than the two from business you mention. That is a majority – use it!

When governors delegate power to committees they must do so responsibly and thoughtfully, not just lie back and let it happen to them. Next time suggest that committees are balanced in their composition with every group represented on all of them. Don't acquiesce in all the powerful functions being grouped in one committee, and remember you don't actually have to delegate *any* power (except on committees which may give rise to appeals, e.g. pupil and teacher discipline) if it is not the majority wish. It is not a good idea in my view to group finance, admissions, curriculum and staffing policy together. It is too big a concentration of power even if the group itself is balanced.

Even more important, it looks as if you may be delegating responsibilities which legally can't be delegated. Curriculum responsibility must be held by the governing body as a whole, for instance, and so must admissions. And make a nuisance of yourselves to get such matters as pupil welfare and community links properly discussed by the governors. They may not be subjects which acquire glamour on your particular governing body, but they *are* important and should have adequate time.

Minority government

Two or three powerful governors dominate our meetings, take agreement for granted or ridicule points made by colleagues. As head this upsets me but I do not think I can do anything about it in my role. Can you advise?

I would guess that many of the decisions your governors make in this situation are illegal, since a power group of this kind will not stop at dominating the discussion but will actually assume powers the governors have not delegated. You do not say whether your chair is among them. I expect he/she is, but if not this is a weak chair and must be encouraged privately by you to prevent this exploitation of the governing body. Emphasize that it is not only dangerous because of the illegality of decisions but also bad for the governors as a team and wasteful of their talents.

If the chair *is* among them, you have to think longer-term, but as I say often, one person cannot restrain abuse of power directly, and permanent solutions require the empowerment of others to deal with it. You have to work on the structures to give more governors tasks and information and therefore confidence. A system for all governors to have regular involvement in the school is a first step, and you can press for this strongly as head because of your conviction that it is the only way to ensure informed decisions shared by all. Then you must seek, stressing your need for support in various aspects of the school's work, the formation of committees and working parties on which all governors are represented. At meetings, remember you are a governor too and every governor should play a part in preventing colleagues being ignored. Any governor can quietly ask for more views to be expressed or question individuals about what they think, so as to open up debate. Finally, as a governor, you have a right to express a view too, remember. I would expect your powerful group to take notice of the head.

Teacher governor drawn into power games

 Our teacher governor never consults the staff about anything coming before governors, nor does he report back on what happened at meetings. He is given regular time off lessons, however, to attend meetings with the chairman and head. We never hear what matters are to be discussed at these meetings and I understand that governors do not know either. Is this common and what do you think about it? Our representative was voted in unopposed.

 The head and chair meet regularly in many schools, in most cases necessarily and with no desire to usurp the role of the governing body. In some cases however other governors dislike it, fearing rightly or wrongly, that things are being 'stitched up' and the governing body manipulated. I have never before heard of a teacher governor being involved in such meetings. I may not have all the facts and there could be some innocent reason, but I must say on the face of it it seems a bit sinister, especially when combined with the fact that your teacher governor feels no obligation to represent you or report back to you. I hope he is not regarded by the head and chair as their mole in the staffroom. Governing bodies are unwise if they tolerate any meetings whose purpose is not made clear to them and which are not reported to the whole group afterwards. I think indeed that they are unwise to tolerate any self-appointed groups which do not have a clear task assigned by the governing body as a whole and which are not open to all.

Individual governors, likewise, are unwise to invite suspicion by joining any such groups. They often feel flattered at being asked to join private discussions and that is when the trouble starts.

But you want to know what *you* can do, not being a governor yourself. As far as the governing body is concerned if you have a friend there, tell him/her what you have told me, and suggest that the governing body ought to concern itself with these meetings of three members and at least ask for a full report of the discussion to be circulated. Even if this were done I still would consider it bad practice, but it is a start. Ideally I believe any meeting of a group of governors, even official committees, should have a clear remit. It is also better in my opinion for all committees to be open to governors other than their core members, as observers.

Within the staffroom you really must introduce the idea that your representative should be expected to be just that, listening to your concerns and reporting back. Why should the purpose of the meetings for which he is given time off be a taboo subject? Any democratic procedure needs the vigilance of those who do the electing and reasonable pressure on the person elected to do the job, if it is to stay healthy. Maybe next time at least the election will be taken more seriously.

Does the vicar always have to be chairman?

 In a voluntary-aided school, is it automatic that the vicar is chairman? I heard our vicar say that he is 'ex-officio' chairman. He is rather ineffective.

 There is no such thing as an ex-officio chairman. Nor is there any requirement to elect the vicar or priest. But when the vicar or priest expects it governors often find it very hard or embarrassing to contemplate electing someone else. Often it will be a very suitable choice and you will acquire someone who cares very much about the school and is prepared to put in a lot of effort. At the other extreme you may have someone who is either too busy with parish affairs or is out of touch with schools as they are now and the increased duties of governors, in which case it will be very difficult for governors to assume their proper role. Only you can say which is the case in your school, and balance the need for change against the risk of causing hurt and ill will. From my travels I would say that the incumbent is chair a little less often than used to be the case, probably because neither job gets any easier.

In any kind of school the choice of chair must not prevent you from doing the job as governors that the law requires, or inhibit team building. It should also not prevent the school developing the more open and effective communication intended by law. In everything we do we should think about the children and their needs. This often makes it easier to do something difficult – when the majority wish it.

A governor with too many irons in the fire

Our chair of governors is conscientious and wants to take part in everything, which is good in itself. He is a solicitor in this little town, however, and several times during his chairmanship issues have come up where his firm (quite small) has been professionally consulted by someone closely involved in the matter. For instance they were retained by a teacher who was involved in an accusation of fraud, and as governors we subsequently had to decide what to do about this teacher pending court proceedings. In another case his firm was asked to advise the parents of an excluded pupil whether they had a good enough case to contest permanent exclusion. He also helped a client who wished to establish a private playgroup in part of our building to draw up proposals. The rest of us thought he should play no part in these discussions of the governors, but he did not agree. Who was right?

I suppose your chair would argue that the firm received fees whatever the outcome of the governors' decision and therefore was no longer financially interested in that outcome. I find that very thin, as you and your colleagues have obviously done. First, a solicitor will have heard the best arguments for the client so starts with one side of the case strongly implanted in his/her mind. This applies to pupils or teachers in trouble. Second, a client like the would-be play-group tenant who succeeds with the help of his/her solicitors (whether or not there has been bias) in getting a favourable decision is more likely to use that firm again, so pecuniary interest comes in. Above all, however, any judicial or business decisions of governors must be seen to be totally beyond reproach, and if there were later any investigation of how a decision was made, the involvement of one party's solicitors would attract comment, even if another partner had handled it. You must be firm as a governing body and insist that your colleague keeps out of these decisions.

Eligibility to be on a selection panel

 We are shortly to appoint a new head and the deputy, who is acting head, will be a very strong candidate. He is the one who as deputy was responsible for the budget. He worked very closely on finances with an administrative assistant who is a co-opted governor. The governors have been arguing a bit about who is to be on the selection panel. Neither of our teacher governors is eligible because they are in one case a faculty head and in another a senior teacher, and they both could well apply for the deputy's post if he were appointed. A majority of governors wish this administrative assistant to be one of our representatives. Partly it is because she is the only 'insider' who is eligible (if of course she is eligible) but she is also an impressive and able woman who would represent us very well and who knows the school and its needs inside out. Several governors are being awkward, arguing both that she is not an educationist and that she is too close to one of the candidates.

 I assume that your colleague wants to be on the selection panel: if she felt uneasy about it herself the governors should of course respect her feelings. Otherwise I see no reason why she should not serve. It seems as if her perspective could be valuable. I do not know the meaning of the remark about not being an educationist. All governors are lay people and governors alone appoint senior staff, though they have professional advice available if they want it. As for the close working relationship, I do not think it constitutes a special personal interest in the outcome of a kind which would disqualify her. Heads, senior staff and governors all have to make decisions sometimes about people they work closely with, and we must all expect our colleagues to show professional detachment, as we should try to do ourselves, following the criteria set for the decision closely and honourably, and thinking about the best interests of the school. Disqualification only arises if the governor concerned or their partner stood to gain from the outcome in a direct sense.

Who manages the money?

 I have heard you talk about not having too many 'men in dark suits' on finance committees, but surely when we have governors with expertise we have to make use of them? I feel very inadequate in business matters, being fully involved in bringing up my family and having - do not yell at me - left serious money matters to my husband who happens to be a man in a dark suit! I can be useful in many other ways, knowing the school well as I do, helping in the classroom, organizing things and supporting pupils' activities.

 I agree that governors have different strengths and we would be mad not to use expertise. It is a matter of degree. The big danger is that if we type-cast governors too much, finance in a school will take on a life of its own. If you have brought up a family you will have managed quite a lot of money. In a school money must be the servant of children's learning and not its master, and from the things you take an interest in you are just the governor to watch this carefully. Similarly, the men in dark suits need to get involved in the classroom a bit if they are to understand what they are doing. The governing body *must* keep hold of the responsibility it shares for the budget and get someone from each interest group on board. If people are making financial decisions seem difficult, treat them with suspicion. A good dark suit person should make financial decisions easier for others.

A good idea: meeting in different classrooms

 I am head of a primary school. I thought it would be a good idea if each governors' meeting took place in a different classroom, which I judged would well repay the effort of getting it ready by giving governors more of a 'feel' for the school and the work going on in it. What do you think?

 I think it is really excellent, and new to me. I immediately think of additional ways of using the idea. Encourage the teacher concerned to take special trouble in preparation for the meeting with a representative display of the class's work and the teaching methods used, and to attend as a visitor so that he/she can point out items of particular interest and say a little about the schemes of work for that year. If the time is suitable you can even have a few pupils in turn come in to show the governors their classroom and perhaps hand round any papers not previously circulated. It all helps make the governors more real to teachers and pupils and the work of the school more real to governors, especially those who can't easily get in during school time. Even those who can visit but are shy should feel easier about coming in during the school day as a result. The idea would help demystify the governing body for teachers and also give them a new perspective on their own work as they think about presenting it to this mixed audience.

How can I remain in touch with the school now my child has left?

I am now a co-opted governor of the primary school where all my children were educated, and in my time I was a parent governor. Now that I no longer have news brought home by the children, see their teachers regularly, have regular written communication, I feel that my understanding of the school is only partial. I am very committed to it and do all I can to keep in touch (I do not have a job), but I dread becoming one of those governors whom I was so hard on when I was a parent governor, the ones who come to meetings in a dark, silent school and know nothing of its daily life. How can I keep my contact? The head does not seem to think it important.

I am sure you under-rate your understanding of the school and the immense experience you bring to it. But you are right in implying that knowledge of it daily affairs is vital.

Can you introduce the idea of a system for every governor to spend time seeing the school at work, either through a duty governor of the month system or attachment to a class or area of work? It might be wise to talk to the head first and get his imagination working on it, and also a few sympathetic governors, before you bring it up formally, since without support it might just run into the sand. Tell the head how you feel and how important it is to the school to have well-informed ambassadors, good understanding between governors and teachers, and decisions which reflect real knowledge. Emphasize that it would be to learn, not to judge.

If this is not acceptable to your colleagues (and it is for governors to decide, not the head in the end) could you not ask for some opportunity to help in the school yourself, either through a regular small chore or stint of classroom assistance, or for particular events (preparing for an open day or special occasion, a sponsored walk, an outing)?

Another idea I can offer is that you suggest the school has a named folder for every governor kept in the school office, into which is slipped routinely any communication that goes out to parents. This literally takes only a few minutes a week, and costs nothing, since governors would come in personally and empty their folders when they can. Newsletters to parents, information about educational visits, clubs, sporting fixtures and rules give an excellent insight into the school day-by-day.

Finally, what about having the governors' meeting in a different classroom each time, and making an event of it in that the class teacher would prepare a special display of that class's work and perhaps attend the meeting for a short time to talk about that class and its affairs?

Spending time in the school

I know you come across many governing bodies where the LEA and business interests are the powerful group, but in ours it is the reverse. Some of us from business feel inhibited because our involvement in the schools is less than that of parent and some co-opted governors who have family connections in the school. They also manage to get into it during the day, and we do not feel able to enter confidently in discussions which depend on knowledge of the school routines and methods and sometimes wish that someone would make a point of using the experience we can offer.

All governors have a responsibility for each other, like any good team, and those who can see clearly how they can be good governors themselves should not neglect those whose potential is not so obvious. But exclusion of others is rarely deliberate, just thoughtless, and you might find it worth while to tell some of your colleagues whom you find approachable, and your head, what you have told me. They may not realize that you feel frustrated.

You surely have some skill to offer which does not require presence in school hours, e.g. sharing experience with parents and older pupils on careers; contributing to governors' work any professional expertise you have on financial or legal matters, marketing, community affairs and resources; writing or organizing skills. They can't know unless you tell them. There may be evening events involving parents where governors' presence all helps to promote understanding, and there will surely be some out-of-school activities (Saturday sporting fixtures, theatre visits, etc.) in which the interest and practical support of governors are invaluable.

Having said this, I hope you are not saying that you can't manage to spend any time during the school day seeing pupils at work, either using some annual leave or persuading your employers that you are performing a public service which many progressive firms support. All schools should have a system for involving governors on some sort of rota in focused and structured activity. This particularly helps those who are less familiar with the school, giving them confidence to contribute in meetings and being good ambassadors in the community they represent.

Specialized training for governors

 I am the head of a grant-maintained school. Would it be possible to devote some of our governor training budget to specialized training for individual governors in, say, finance, law, building matters? We are anxious to develop a strong foundation of expertise in these important subjects.

 I am sure there is no reason why you should not spend whatever your governing body as a whole and your school community in general think desirable on such training. I put it this way because I can imagine there would be different views about it. However ample your budget there will always be uses of money in a school which constitute keen competition and which will have their passionate advocates. What is more your other governors might feel that their development as an effective team is also an important claim on available funds. But assuming they think specialist training for a few of their number is a reasonable thing to aim at, I know of no technical objection.

I have answered your question, and I expect you will guess that I would not be enthusiastic about such an idea if it came up on a governing body of which I was a member. To me the whole point of governors is that they are not specialists. They learn a great deal about all sorts of things along the way, but among those things I do not see certain kinds of expertise as being of a different order of importance. After all the primary business of a school governing body is education, yet no-one suggests that they go on a BEd course so that they understand what teachers are aiming at. It is only money and law and buildings that people seem so keen to make mysteries about, and money particularly, which everybody manages at some level. The danger is that finance will become an end in itself instead of a means, and that those who acquire that expertise will play a bigger part in decisions on school priorities than the rest of the team, at the expense of unity.

Spending a training budget

 In our LEA we have a chance to use about two-thirds of our delegated training money to 'buy back' a basic training programme. Special events - involving an outside speaker, say - will have to be paid for. We shall certainly accept the basic package, which is good value, and I even think some of my colleagues (I am a keen parent governor/chair, sometimes irritated by a few who are less keen) will be more inclined to accept training now that we pay. My question is about the pathetically small sum of money we have left, about £5 per governor per year. Is there anything useful we can do with this apart from join in one of the events I spoke of?

 There is a good choice of things to spend that sort of sum on. You could invest in a basic stock of books (your training co-ordinator will advise you on titles) for your governing body, and/or subscribe to one or more journals for your own use - the *Times Educational Supplement, Education, Managing Schools Today, Governors' Action, ACE Bulletin, Parents and Schools.* (Again your co-ordinator will give you details.) You could join Action for Governors' Information and Training, the National Association of Governors and Managers or the Campaign for State Education and get their literature regularly.

You could organize workshops for yourselves geared to your own concerns: leaders from within the education system need not cost anything. Joining with other neighbouring schools would make more ambitious events possible and you would also benefit from sharing experience. You could spend money on modest hospitality for your teachers (one governing body made it breakfast) to enable you to get to know them, learn from them, and discuss school affairs in a relaxed atmosphere without the pressure of a formal agenda. This works wonders for relationships and so, if you can manage it, does getting away somewhere for 24 hours as a governing body to think more fundamentally about your job than is normally possible. I know the money will not stretch to that, but I heard of one governing body which got sponsorship to help fund such an event.

Finally, in addition to joining with neighbouring schools' governors, think about whether you could combine your resources with some of your school's staff in-service budget for a training event from which both governors and staff would benefit. Maybe as you say less enthusiastic colleagues will use more actively any facilities they have helped to choose and this will in the long run lead to their also valuing more the excellent service most LEA training teams provide.

9 Change and challenge

When I next collect governors' questions into a book, I feel sure that it is this chapter, not 1, 6 or 8, which will be the one which is bursting at the seams and having to be radically pruned. The changes heralded by the Schools Act 1992 and the Education Act 1993 are slow to impinge on the service, but they will affect it profoundly.

Four-yearly inspections, action plans, failing schools. Governors will soon be in on the act at school level with a vengeance. Then there is the massive structural change envisaged by the 1993 Act, under which the strategic control of education will be shared with LEAs in many areas by a government-appointed funding council, empowered to establish new schools, initiate changes in the character of existing grant-maintained schools, and welcome independently promoted schools into the grant-maintained sector.

Meanwhile, governors struggle to keep a steady course, support and advance the interests of their own schools, fumble for what they used to recognize as a public service code of practice and belief. Some of them are already heavily into the grant-maintained argument, either for themselves or because the decisions of neighbours have forced it upon them. A proportion have already been inspected, and some are realizing what it means to be accountable for processes you have not had much genuine involvement in yet. This will raise consciousness very quickly. I expect there to be a great deal of heart-searching in the wake of OFSTED into the real part to be played by governors, with perhaps a sharpening of the focus on governors in the inspection itself. Governors are beginning to organize themselves into many local and national associations, and perhaps sooner than we think will find a voice for themselves and perhaps win a say in how the service is to be organized in future. They will continue to get better at seeing their schools through change and challenge, at involving themselves in the processes of school improvement, and whatever the future holds we can be certain that things will never be the same again. Governors are surely here to stay.

Is a grant-maintained school a state school?

 I have been arguing with another governor whose child attends a grant-maintained school about the status of that school. She refers to it as a 'private' school, because the premises and all the facilities belong to the school, because it is independent of the council and because admission is by interview. It also, by the way, gives itself airs in the form of a fancy new uniform and a house system. I say a private school is one which charges fees. Can you settle this dispute?

 The question 'what is a state school?' has become a more difficult one now that dependence on public funds has been divorced to some degree from ownership and control. However, I am firmly on your side. A state school to me is one which is wholly funded from public money and is free to the user. After all voluntary-aided schools also own their buildings and have some say in whom they admit, and this has been so for many years. Many publicly provided schools have strict uniforms and house systems. Grant-maintained schools are answerable in the end to central government, they are obliged to teach the national curriculum (which private schools are not) and the composition of their governing bodies and many of their working practices are laid down in legislation. Incidentally if you suspect that a local grant-maintained school is operating a form of selection which is not in keeping with the character of the school as it was before, you should look into it. This is not proper.

Like many others I find it hard to accept that public money should be used to maintain schools which are not subject to the kind of local democratic controls we have been used to, but I also think we do more to maintain democratic principles if we do not put up unnecessary barriers, if we go on debating issues of service, co-operation and accountability with all local schools, and sharing ideas and good practices. This is particularly important for governors to play their part in, since whatever the future holds it is in all our interests that the pupils and parents in grant-maintained schools have the benefits of open, democratic and effective school government.

A head teacher's part in the opting-out debate

 What do you think should be the role of the head teacher when discussing grant-maintained status? I know heads who have favoured the move and done a great deal to bring it about. I have argued with them that this is wrong and that it could undermine them professionally if in spite of their efforts grant-maintained status fails to gain enough parental support. But those heads who are pro-grant-maintained status say that without them the debate would never take off, and that it is their duty to put before staff, parents and governors the benefits which the school would gain. Now I find myself confused. Some of my governors wish to encourage a ballot. Frankly I think it could result in a vote for grant-maintained status if the arguments against are not aired, and my view of the school's long-term well-being and place in the community makes it hard for me to contemplate such an outcome.

 It is always easier to be detached if what you want to happen is likely to happen without you! This is one problem you share with your pro-grant-maintained status colleagues. But I am sure none the less that heads who exceed their legal role in the opting-out debate face grave dangers, graver I think if they are in favour, simply because they are then advocating a major departure from the status quo, and those who support change always have the greater obligation to prove that it will be for the better. I have known cases where the head has taken a strong pro-grant-maintained status line throughout, and has suffered some trauma professionally as a result of losing the vote.

Whatever the head's views, however, you cannot escape the fact that legally the head has no role at all to influence the outcome of the parents' ballot. If the head is a governor, he/she does at least participate in the governors' decision to go to ballot or not. At that governors' meeting the head, like any other governor, is entitled to express views freely, and if you judge it right you can certainly put forward the moral/community arguments about which you feel strongly, and can also counter arguments based on the likely benefits to the school if you consider them unsound. But if a majority vote to go to ballot, that is the end of it and you must abide by their decision. Similarly you must do nothing to discourage parents who clearly want a ballot.

After that I think a head's role is to ensure that parents have the benefit of all the information available and are exposed to a wide range of opinions on either side. What you feel inside should not be allowed to stop you getting pro-grant-maintained status speakers at a meeting, and a head who is pro-grant-maintained status should bend over backwards to make sure that parents hear the arguments against. So often I get complaints that the head has restricted access to other points of view. You would be super-human if you did not respond to a direct question about your opinion or that of the staff, but you should remind those who ask that neither you nor the staff have any legal part in the process and that you would continue to do your best for the school whatever parents decided. In extremes I realize that that might include resignation, but that is a weapon which I would consider it quite improper to use in the debate.

A school in trauma following a vote against opting out

Our school balloted on whether to apply to become grant-maintained. The parental vote went against it by a heavy majority. Now we are settling down to normal life again, but the process has been divisive. It has set parents against parents, teachers against teachers, and even the governors, who had been divided on going to ballot, are not the friendly group we used to be. Where there was trust and common purpose, there is now suspicion and resentment. Above all the head, who made it almost a vote of confidence in himself and got deeply involved, is a different person – morose and negative. Neighbour schools are wary and hostile. How can we make a fresh start?

It will take time. Whatever the merits or otherwise of grant-maintained status the *process* is nearly always divisive. The most serious problem you have is the head. I always advise heads as you know that they should avoid getting too involved personally (they have no legal role, except as a member of the governing body), since the effect of losing, after making it a matter of confidence, is likely to be professional trauma. He needs your help now, and the governors must be firm and explicit in their support for him, for the school's sake, making it clear that the chapter is closed and the school's work goes on. Never lose a chance to talk about the things which are special about it or an opportunity to use the real choices given to us by LMS to make imaginative moves. Help the head in every way you can to restore his confidence. Those of you who were against GMS must make a special effort to show friendship and solidarity with those who lost the argument. I think it would be a good plan for the governors to meet all the staff, to emphasize that there must be unity now, preferably with some clear initiatives to discuss for the future. Pay special attention to frequent and positive communication with parents during this time to show them that the school is in good heart, and join in any local discussion forums with other schools as if nothing had happened: it will take time to build up the relationships again but any evidence that you feel concerned for the local service as a whole will help.

Finally, when a school has run into any crisis of morale I always recommend trying to find some 'giant spectacular' which generates a lot of energy and involves the whole school community or perhaps even other local schools as well – a pageant, local history project, effort for an appealing cause.

A church school looks at grant-maintained status

 As a voluntary-aided school governing body we were initially most reluctant to go for grant-maintained status. We would not consider it now except for the relief of the 15% we have to pay for outside repairs and improvements. It is a poor parish, and the school is very old and makes heavy demands on our church funds even for essential repairs, and the kind of modernization we have dreamed of seems out of reach. To be frank we think the government's policy is just a way of tempting schools like ours to go grant-maintained perhaps against their principles. We are especially concerned about our relationships with other schools in a very deprived area. Perhaps it is not fair to ask you, but we wonder whether even this inducement will be withdrawn once it is done its job?

 I can't answer that question of course. All I can say is that the concession is now part of the law and it would not be that simple to change it. On the other hand, it is only right to point out, if you don't know, that there can be no guarantee that you get your work authorized. Your requests will be in competition with other grant-maintained schools, not as now with other voluntary-aided schools able to pay their share. That brings us to the question nobody can yet answer, which is what capital funds will be available for the grant-maintained sector in the long term. I assume you have discussed the matter fully with your diocese and will take account of their advice as well as exploring fully what help they can give.

It would be wrong for me to comment here on the political issue you raise. The grant-maintained option is a fundamental part of government strategy and each school must respond in its own way. I know many potential applicants for grant-maintained status have the same worries as you do about relationships with other schools, but I myself can only feel sympathy with governors faced with such very difficult decisions and could never blame them for the choice they made. I believe many people have this basic understanding. The aspect of the situation which does make me angry – and it goes far beyond the immediate issue of opting out – is that because investment in the maintenance and improvement of school premises has been inadequate for so long, schools are forced into decisions which have nothing to do with the issue of grant-maintained status as such. I should see the policy in a different light if schools were able to take this step only because they had conviction about the educational benefits of grant-maintained status and knew how they were going to use their extra independence for the benefit of children's learning. From where I stand it seems as if these are a minority of those who opt out, and the rest are motivated by despair over getting funding for their needs, by fear of closure or change, or by the knock-on effect of other schools' decisions.

How can I remain a governor of a grant-maintained school?

Our school has just become grant-maintained. I did my very best to prevent this outcome because I think it is divisive and indeed I fought it right to the end. It is not a political matter for me: I am a parent governor and have had many years of association with the school. Do I now have to accept the majority decision? I know you always say governors must be loyal to corporate decisions but I find it so hard not to show my feelings and even to refrain from telling people what fools I think they were.

I sympathize, but I cannot give you any different answer. Governing bodies can only work effectively if their decisions once made are robust, and that means united. If you do not feel you can put the argument behind you and work wholeheartedly for the school's success in its new life then I am afraid you ought to resign as a governor. If you are very deeply committed to the school – and it sounds as if you are – you can perhaps reflect on the fact that it is still a state school and still your local school with the same parents, teachers and children associated with it. If you have doubts about grant-maintained status as a system you will also be concerned about the principles and values by which your school operates and about the fair treatment of those teachers, children and parents once the protection of the local authority is removed. Who better to speak up for what is right than you – if you can?

A school coping with a grant-maintained neighbour

 Grant-maintained status for a neighbouring school has given us a crop of problems. First, our numbers have been down, with pupils taken from our very doorstep and obvious financial consequences. The grant-maintained school has gone in for a smart uniform, expensively designed letterheads, fairly heavy discipline policies (which incidentally mean among other things a lot of excluded pupils who often end up with us – we scarcely ever exclude), and these things seem to attract parents. We also think they are selecting pupils both by interview and on the basis of reports from previous schools, hard to prove when they are heavily oversubscribed. (Is it legal?) One does not hear much about special needs provision and if a child has a problem or disability parents are advised to send them to a school which 'has the facilities'. So if we get the reputation of taking all comers, having discipline problems, being short of money, what next? Parents feel that they are almost getting private education down the road, and are even asked for an annual contribution for school funds. Do we try to beat them or join them? If we fall below a viable size will the new funding council have power to close us? How will the 1993 Act in general affect us?

 You have listed all the possible divisive consequences of grant-maintained status. On your last two questions, the new funding councils only have planning powers (i.e. including the closure of schools) when the number of primary or secondary opted-out schools in an area reaches 75%. That has not yet happened in your LEA area, but the 1993 Act does in various ways aim to making opting out easier. These include requiring consideration of grant-maintained status by governors every year, abolishing the requirement for a second meeting of governors, and limiting what can be spent on putting the case against opting out. The Act also allows the establishment of new grant-maintained schools which could both change the market situation and hasten the growth to 75%, and it encourages the removal of surplus places. Changes which may help you on the other hand are that LEAs may direct a school, even a grant-maintained school, to take any pupil who has not secured a place and also an excluded pupil, and LEAs and funding councils share in the transitional stage responsibility for non-statemented pupils with special needs (LEAs retain jurisdiction over the statemented sector.) There are provisions strengthening special needs arrangements, including an appeals tribunal and a code of practice.

On the various points you raise about the competition being mounted by your neighbouring grant-maintained school, we have to accept that the creation of this form of competition is the law of the land and a major element in government policy. Other schools will think hard about how to respond and in my view it can only help matters to maintain contact and keep public service issues alive in the local debate. We can at least be vigilant about any possible breaches in the law which render the competition unfair. For instance a grant-maintained school is obliged to keep the same general character, including, e.g., being non-selective. As you say, however, it is difficult to prove selection, and in any case the schools can apply for permission to change and the Secretary of State has already approved various degrees of selection in a number of individual GM schools. Watch for any real evidence that back-door selection takes place. Also grant-maintained schools have no more right than LEA schools to make charges for what they provide, and if there is any suggestion that the contribution to funds is more than voluntary, follow it up. Finally, grant-maintained schools still have the same obligations to cater for special needs as LEA schools, and we should make sure they accept them.

On the general issue of beat-them-or-join-them, remember that any school, grant-maintained or not, is at liberty to provide (within the law and the constraints of the national curriculum) whatever it thinks will attract parents. But in the part of your letter I have not quoted, you make it clear that you as governors are proud of your school as it is, and don't wish to change what you feel are educationally good policies just to keep up with the Joneses. That is right, and provided a school is not complacent and looks regularly at itself to ensure it communicates well with parents and is not clinging to stale and self-righteous postures in the name of educational principles, I would back it 100% in not selling its soul for privileges.

But principles should represent a positive attitude and be worth advertising. Too often those who represent values currently under attack are defeatist about them or think there is something intrinsically wrong with salesmanship. It depends what kind of selling tactics. Glossy publicity may work in the short term, but in the end a school's best advertisement are its hundreds of pupils and parents, who are interested in the contents of the jar, not the label. I believe a school should market vigorously those features which no school can take away from another, namely its localness and the associated responsiveness to parents and community. If it promises to meet all needs to the best of its ability, parents can easily be shown that any child may at some time need extra help, go through a bad patch or get into trouble. If it promises to be patient and tolerant at such times, and work in close collaboration with parents, there are few who would not trade choice for influence and understand that if you go for choice you may not have the easy access which a neighbourhood school provides. In short, if you believe in your policies there is no need to be apologetic about them.

Opting out: the rights of other schools affected to express views

A comprehensive in our area plans to opt out. The proposal is tearing the community apart, since the consequences for other schools could be serious. Parents and teachers associated with other secondary schools and feeder primary schools are talking and writing about it and trying to persuade others of the folly of it. This surely is part of any democratic process, but the parents of the opt-out lobby in the school concerned are pursuing opponents relentlessly, asking them whether they are parents of XYZ School, asking what business it is of theirs, implying that we have no right to an opinion. Have we no moral right to be concerned?

Of course you have. Many indeed think it wrong that future parents do not have a voice in the ballot itself, and in particular argue that parents whose children will shortly move to the school should have a vote rather than those whose children will have left before the change takes place. However the law has decreed otherwise. It does nevertheless recognize the interests of future parents, competing schools, and others affected by the change, by providing for any school or any ten local government electors to lodge objections once the application has been made to the Secretary of State. To try to limit the debate beforehand is like saying that if you have just moved to a town and are not yet on the electoral roll you cannot have a view on the siting of a new supermarket!

Opting out: the right to have parents' addresses

 I am a parent at a school which is going to ballot on opting out. I happen to be against it, and a few of us have formed an action committee to fight the idea. We find that parents have only been given one side of the case, and we want to have a meeting at which other arguments can be brought out. For this purpose we have asked the headmistress if we can have a list of parents' names and addresses, but she has refused. Is she allowed to do this? She is in favour of opting out and so are most of the governors, and I think we are being muzzled.

 You are entitled to have the names and addresses. This is covered by Section 60(7) of the Education Reform Act 1988. The governing body of a school where a ballot is proposed must on request provide any parent of a registered pupil with the names and addresses of other parents. The list may be inspected free of charge but if you want a copy of the list for yourself the governors may make a charge not exceeding the cost of copying it. The details of any parents who have specifically objected to having them disclosed – as they are legally entitled to – must be excluded, however.

Teachers' rights when a school opts out

 As a teacher in a school opting out, I had no say in the decision. I have conscientious objections to teaching in a grant-maintained school. Have I a right to another posting?

 I am afraid not. The law is clear on the matter. Local authorities vary in their attitude to the whole process, but many will do their best to help teachers with problems even though not obliged to employ them.

Preparing for OFSTED

 We have no date yet for our first inspection under the new arrangements, but want to be ready. How can we as governors best prepare? It is a good comprehensive school, with well above average achievement. Some of us think it does not do so well by the less academic and our truancy and exclusion figures are on the high side by comparison with some of our less academic competitors.

 I am sure you have access to information on the basic requirements, and your head must be busily collecting books and articles from educational magazines which you can borrow. Your LEA governor support unit may also have guidelines/ training. I shall concentrate on less obvious points and those particularly concerning governors.

First, take a look at the list of documents which inspectors will take away with them before they begin. I guess you will be quite shocked. Not just obvious things like the prospectus and the development plan, schemes of work and other curriculum documents, but all governors' written policies, recent minutes, your annual report to parents (if another is due before the inspection now is your chance to give its quality a higher priority) and recent heads' reports to governors. (Again if you think yours leaves something to be desired you have a good reason to say so now and ask for one which better meets your information needs.) Remember too that for the first time the work of governors will be a major part of the inspectors' remit and apart from any deficiencies in your written work you must use what time you have looking honestly at relationships between school and governors and ask what can be improved. Remember however that inspectors will be very alert to hastily-cobbled policies and papered-over tensions, and it is far better to be found thoughtfully and honestly working on problems if they can't be genuinely solved in the time you have.

This last bit of advice applies of course to the basic problem you have mentioned in your school. Where such a problem exists it is usually of long standing and you should expect – indeed hope – that it will be picked up and taken seriously. You must welcome guidance on long-term improvements: these will clearly figure largely in your post-inspection action plan.

In a school with high achievers and indices of disaffection you will obviously look first at the curriculum. What are its current targets? If it aims mainly to provide a good number of outstanding results and maximize the proportion with five subjects at Grades A to C – the accepted measure – it will take certain actions which are different from another school which aims only to reduce the proportion leaving without qualifications. A third school might concentrate on getting almost all leavers passes in the three core subjects, and a fourth might try to push D and E grades up to C. You are right: schools don't have such narrow aims and they will all have written down somewhere that they aim to develop the maximum potential in every child. But when you scratch the surface you will find differences of focus all the same. Then you will dig deeper and look at exam board and syllabus choices, examination entry policy, ability groupings, options, less academic alternatives and all sorts of other curriculum levers. You will also look at out-of-class activities. I deliberately did not say 'extra-curricular', because if your object is to spread achievement you will see all the experience the school offers as part of the strategy. Look at your discipline guidelines as well. Are they about *good* behaviour as well as punishment for bad? Is your provision for special needs good, and your pastoral care?

A few more points. It might be an idea if there is time for the school to enlist the help of your LEA inspectors/advisers, through the one attached to your school if you have that system. Second, remember that the inspectors will have a meeting with parents before they begin, and if there are any tensions between parents and the school or any unresolved problems in the relationship, it would be wise to look at them now.

Finally and above all, be honest among yourselves and with your head about your own feelings and also talk a lot about the features of your school you are all most proud of. Make sure that you don't play down the good things in looking for possible areas of criticism, especially in your contacts with staff. It could otherwise be a negative experience for them and this would be the worst possible outcome. Honesty about shortcomings is good but not at the expense of pride and confidence.

Do OFSTED inspectors have to meet governors beforehand?

 We have our date for the OFSTED inspection. Do inspectors have to meet governors beforehand? Nothing has been said to us.

 There is no written requirement to meet governors, but the latest guidelines encourage it. Since the inspection has to include the management of the school and the part played by governors, and in view of governors' major involvement in much of what the inspectors will be reporting on and in the subsequent action plan, it is highly desirable. You as governors can take the initiative and ask for a meeting. Whether it is with the whole governing body, just the chair, or some number in between, is for negotiation between yourselves and the inspecting team.

OFSTED and the effectiveness of governors

 If a head teacher's involvement of governors in the running of the school is judged by OFSTED inspectors to be insufficient, what is the next step?

 I do not know whether this is a theoretical question based on wishful thinking, or has actually happened! Certainly the OFSTED inspectors are meant to include the working of the governing body and can comment on its relationships with all partners. I doubt whether many teams spend a great deal of time on this from what I have heard so far. Governors can ask for an opportunity to talk to the inspectors if a meeting is not automatically set up, and there is no reason why they should not voice any concerns which have a bearing on the management of the school. If the report comments on problems in this area it does help governors who have not previously been able to establish a proper partnership, even if the issue is not highlighted. But if the matter is picked out as a point for special attention, the governors themselves can scarcely avoid grasping the nettle and setting out in their action plan how they will proceed.

This will be a critical moment for those governing bodies. They can either fudge it and produce a few meaningless expressions of intent, or they can set out as a detailed agenda the most important areas for improvement. This statement could include a programme of work related to major decisions required at particular times of year - the budget, admissions, options, minor capital works - to ensure their involvement in time. It could envisage the setting up of committees and working parties, call for the introduction of a system for all governors to make planned and structured visits to the school, and set out the information they need to do their work, including that in the head's report. The plan must in short be precise. We are talking of a minority of schools where things are really bad – perhaps because of the governors' own lack of direction or because they have been restricted in their role by others – and they will not have a better chance to improve matters than OFSTED affords.

What if we are classed a failing school?

 Everybody in this school is fearful of being classified as a failing school. Do not misunderstand, we think our school does wonders in its community, that the staff are dedicated and skilled and that children from poor backgrounds get all the support and understanding that is humanly possible. But on SATS scores and the general standards of the pupils we could not be compared with a school in a more favoured situation. If the worst happened could we apply to become a grant-maintained school to avoid closure?

 The formal answer to your question is that once a school has been designated for special measures it cannot ballot for grant-maintained status. After it has been run for a period by an Education Association it is again inspected and on the result of this the Secretary of State decides whether it should close or become grant-maintained (return to its former status is not at this stage an option).

But please, everybody, don't meet trouble halfway. First, the inspectors will take full account of the circumstances of your school and indeed the framework within which OFSTED inspections take place specifically provide for the nature of the community served by the school to be studied at the outset. Provided it is judged that the school's expectations of its pupils are not too low, their achievement will be seen in the light of the local circumstances. Second, even when a school has an adverse report there is an opportunity for its governors (if it has a delegated budget) or the LEA to take measures to remedy shortcomings revealed in the report, and it is only if these are considered by the Secretary of State to be ineffective that the Education Association comes in.

Your confidence in your teachers and your pride in what the school does in difficult circumstances will shine through in all your contact with the inspecting team and these are the greatest gifts you can offer. Try in the meantime to build up staff morale by remembering to express these feelings, talking a good deal about achievements and trying to make teachers feel positive about what they are doing.

Improving a poor department

 What can we do about a department, in our case modern languages, which is persistently under-performing? I emphasize that I mean this in every sense: poor exam results by comparison both with other schools, other faculties in the school and its own past best, and deteriorating every year, with clear evidence that pupils do not enjoy the lessons. Parents complain about patchy homework setting and marking and failure to progress course work, and now increasingly on dull teaching. Even the exchange visits are poorly planned. The faculty head, promoted from within the faculty, was an excellent class teacher and is not lazy, but seems to have no managerial skills at all, does not develop staff, inject ideas or enthuse pupils. She even fails sometimes to order books for which funding has been authorized. I am sure she wants to do better, but she irritatingly blames the fact that the school has a policy of mixed ability groups, so there are problems with some less able and poorly motivated pupils, and also the quality of the staff we can attract in an expensive housing area.

You clearly have not yet had your OFSTED inspection which will certainly home in on such an obvious problem. You should be seen to have recognized it and to be working on it.

A good school will have a rolling programme of appraisal of each department, with full involvement of *all* staff in self-review. It will also have a curriculum working party of governors who familiarize themselves with each faculty in turn and share fully in concerns which arise. Even where there is a problem and everybody seems sure who it is, it is important that problems are discussed, ideas contributed and solutions 'owned' by all staff, not just the one perceived to be the centre of the trouble – and it is rare for there to be only one person capable of better performance! There should also be a whole-school system of monitoring homework and course-work, and timetables should build in for faculty heads enough time to monitor teaching.

Probably things have gone so far now that you need the LEA's subject adviser(s) to look at the faculty, identifying the problems, counselling, suggesting better ways of monitoring teacher performance, in-service training, differentiated programmes for the less able and perhaps considering setting. (Has you faculty head argued for setting in school policy discussions? Or is it just an excuse she's only now thought of?) As for teacher quality, house prices must affect equally the staff in other faculties and other local schools.

People do get over-promoted and we should be super-careful when appointing to senior posts to probe management skills, though these can be learnt: there must be a suitable management course for middle managers your staff member could attend. You can also relieve her of one or two things she does not do well. Any staff member with organizational skills could take on ordering supplies and perhaps one with imagination as well be given the planning of trips. Check that the faculty head has enough non-contact time to monitor teaching quality and uses it well. Assuming you have thought of everything and are still stuck with a faculty head who after appraisal and with all the support, training and guidance that is available and the use of non-threatening procedures for target-setting and self-review, is still not making it, you are in trouble. Teachers may revert to a lower grade while having their pension based on pay at the time of reversion: this could be one solution in cases where the staff member recognizes the problem and wants to take this route, but it can only be on a voluntary basis.

You may in the end be faced with last-resort procedures leading
to possible dismissal which are slow, hazardous and stressful
for all, but if it does come to this make sure you have done
everything by the book and get the LEA's full support.

A school that is ticking over, and another under-performing faculty

*Our head is away sick and may be off some time. Things are ticking
over under an acting head who was one of our deputies, the one
responsible for the budget and personnel matters, but obviously it is
not easy to get any big problems faced. The school had begun last autumn
on an investigation of our humanities faculty which had performed far
below others in exams year after year, where pupils cut more lessons
and where an abnormally small number go on to A level. The head was
involving governors - cautiously - in some of his thinking and we were
making progress. Now the whole issue seems to be in danger of being
dropped, and as chair I feel we owe it to parents to keep at it. The trouble
is that the head of the faculty, who in my personal view has been over-
promoted and is not managing the team well, or very energetic, has
used the head's absence to drag his feet and obstruct any further work
on their problems. The acting head is not a strong person in dealing
with unpleasantness and seems to be ducking the issue.*

It is good to hear of a governing body keeping its eye on the
important things even in a difficult time for the school. It seems
from the rest of your letter that it is a big school and that there
are two other deputies. In these circumstances the absence of
the head is no excuse for not proceeding with this important
issue, which I would certainly see as one for governors'
involvement. After all if you were to have your OFSTED
inspection next month, the inspectors would certainly pick up
this weakness, highlight it in their report and expect *you* to come
up with a plan. Incidentally for the benefit of other governors I
would add that it is an enormous help if governors have a
curriculum working party which reviews the work of the school
on a Forth Bridge basis. They build up knowledge of the factors
affecting quality and it makes it easier if an area of work at any
time needs special measures. I would also add that in this subject
area you do need to look at the *management* of the faculty

carefully. If it were science or modern languages the factors could be more complex, but humanities has not suffered much from shortage of basically good teachers, and many pupils when well taught normally enjoy the lessons and can thrive in a mixed ability setting. There are other curriculum areas which are much more prone to teacher shortage and more difficult to teach interestingly to all pupils.

Your acting head, understandably enough, is not looking for problems. But I would guess that it would take only a little nudge to touch his conscience - he knows it is important. A key person is the deputy responsible for the curriculum and you should tactfully try to get him/her on your side. At some stage you will need to involve your LEA subject adviser but obviously you want to gain general acceptance first that this is needed.

Indeed as I have recently said to another governor you must try to involve the whole staff of the faculty together in sharing ideas on the way forward. It does not help to focus only on the senior person even when you suspect that most of the trouble is there, and it is important that all are committed to improvement, and feel ownership of the ideas which emerge. In any case there will certainly be ways in which responsibilities can be redistributed to build on strengths. Often faculty heads get landed with jobs they are no good at and that another person could take on, one obvious example being researching and ordering books and equipment. Second, do look at the non-contact time available to faculty heads to monitor lesson quality. This examination may take you into many other aspects of school resource use – class size, minority subjects, possible top-heavy administration – but it will also emphasize the importance of such monitoring in a way which does not appear threatening to the staff member concerned. Remember always that except in an extreme case the show will have to be run by mostly the same people.

Head teachers' rights when schools are amalgamated

 A tentative proposal has been made that our infants school be amalgamated with the junior school on the same site when our head takes early retirement next year and the junior head takes up a post in a much bigger school. We already share a governing body. The chair has ruled that the heads should be excluded from discussion of the matter by the governing body on the ground of personal interest. Is this right?

 I can think of no justification for such exclusion. Neither head is likely to apply for the post in the combined school. Once the decision to amalgamate has been made, the two heads are specifically entitled by reason of Regulation 11(2) of Statutory Instrument 1503 of 1989 to attend meetings of the caretaker governing body until a new head is appointed. This attendance is of course subject to the provisions on withdrawal from any items where the head in question has a direct pecuniary interest.

Useful addresses

Action for Governors Information and Training (AGIT),
Lyng Hall,
Blackberry Lane,
Coventry CV2 3JS
Tel: 01203-638679   Fax: 01203-681161

Advisory Council for Education (ACE),
1B Aberdeen Studios,
22 Highbury Grove,
London N5 2DQ
Tel: 0171-354-8318   Fax: 0171-354-9069

Campaign for State Education (CASE),
158 Durham Road,
London SW20 0DG
Tel/fax: 0181-944-8206

Grant Maintained Schools Foundation (GMSF),
36 Great Smith Street,
London SW1 3BU
Tel: 0171-233-4666 Fax: 0171-339-2795

Institute for School and College Governors (ISCG),
Avondale Park School,
Sirdar Road,
London W11 4EE
Tel: 0171-229-0200 Fax: 0171-229-0651

National Association of Governors and Managers (NAGM),
21 Bennetts Hill,
Birmingham B2 5QP
Tel/fax: 0121-643-5787

National Governors Council,
Simon Goodenough,
Glebe House,
Church Street,
Crediton

Reading lists

Other guides by the same author

Basics for School Governors'   Network Educational Press, 1993.

The Effective School Governor
  Regularly updated, from ACE as delow.

Free for All
  A brief history of state education from the earliest days to the present, with summaries of all recent legislation. By post from Campaign for State Education, 158 Durham Road, London SW20 0DG.

Heads and Governors: Building the Partnership, AGIT, 1994
  By post only from AGIT, Lyng Hall, Blackberry Lane, Coventry, CV3 3JS.

How Schools Work: A really simple guide for governors and parents, 1995
  Available from Advisory Centre for Education (ACE), 1B Aberdeen Studios, 22 Highbury Grove, London N5 2EA.

School Governors: Your Questions Answered, Hodder and Stoughton, 1990.
  Does, of course, need to be read in conjunction with later legislation, but most themes still current.

Schools Parents and Governors: A New Approach to Accountability, Routledge, 1988.

Working Together: Rules and Good Practices for School Governors.
  Written in conjunction with Northamptonshire Governor Services, Russell House, Rickyard Road, The Arbours, Northampton, NN3 3QZ. May be available from your LEA.

Publications from AGIT

School governors and Inspection, Charles Stiles, 1994.
This booklet describes governors'responsibilities for inspection and the ways in which governors' work is considered by inspection. In doing so the author draws out the importance of governing policies and sets out governors' responsibilities for taking action on the report. The booklet offers a suggested checklist which will help governors manage their part in the inspection process.

Staff Pay Policies: Updated Guidance for Governing Bodies, 1993.
This booklet provides guidance on how to prepare a whole school pay policy and includes a sample pay policy. It also provides a clear summary of the new pay legislation 1993 with an insert relating to changes introduced in 1994.

A Whole School Pay Policy: Questions and Answers Through the Eyes of Governors, 1993.
This booklet sponsored jointly by NAGM and AGIT is written for governors of schools with delegated powers under the 1988 Education Act. It deals with the complex issues of paying the school's staff by providing answers to the sort of questions that governors involved with the local management of schools are asking. The subject is looked at through the eyes of governors but this book will also be of interest to others in schools and local authorities.

School Governors' Do-it-better guides
How to Write School Policies
This six– page guide offers step-by-step guidance on how a governing body can play its part in the production of school policy. It contains a checklist of school policies distinguishing between those that are legally required, others that school inspectors may ask to see and some additional policies that we regard as good practice.

Considering Grant Maintained Status
An informative four page guide which lists issues to consider, compares county, voluntary–aided and grant–maintained schools and provides signposts for governors to obtain further information.

How Effective is our Governing Body? 1992
A pack for the self-appraisal of the governing body. These materials produced jointly by AGIT and NAGM have been devised so that governing bodies, who have a vitally important role to play in the education system, can take a look at themselves, decide whether they are working an effective way and set targets for the future.

Photocopiable materials enable all governors to evaluate and comment on the performance of the governing body in a structured way. The whole exercise should take most governors no more than two hours per year but a small group of governors who will organize the process will take an additional three hours.

Governors' Action
A bi-monthly magazine for the working governor.

Stop Press
A monthly summary of educational developments relevant to governing and managing schools.

All the above publications are available from: Action for Governors' Information and Training, Lyng Hall, Blackberry Lane, Coventry CV2 3JS. Tel: 01203-638679 Fax: 01203-681161

Other publications

ACE Governors' Handbook, ACE, 1994.

ACE Special Education Handbook, ACE 1994.

Governors' Guide to the Law, DFE, updated (free).

Governors' Manual, Croner Publications.

Home and School Links, CASE.

School Governors: Policies, Issues and Practices, Terry Mahoney, Macmillan, 1988.

Special Educational Needs: Support for Governors, ACE 1994.

Summary of the 1993 Act, Rick Rogers, ACE.

Index

Universities challenged.

THE TIMES HIGHER EDUCATION SUPPLEMENT

Subscribe now and secure your future copies.

Every week The Times Higher Education Supplement
examines the issues and asks the questions that matter to everyone
with an interest in higher education.
Available at your newsagent or, if you would like to subscribe, please
send a cheque or credit card details to
THES Subscriptions, PO Box 14, Harold Hill, Romford RM3 8EQ, or
call our credit card hotline on 0708 378379.
Annual rates (52 issues): UK £45; Europe and Eire £83; USA and
Canada (Air Freight) US$99; Rest of The World (airmail) £97.

AT NEWSAGENTS · EVERY FRIDAY